Union Public Library
1980 Morris Avenue
Union, N.J. 07083

MULTICULTURAL VOICES

HISPANIC-AMERICAN WRITERS

MULTICULTURAL VOICES

AFRICAN-AMERICAN WRITERS

ARAB-AMERICAN AND MUSLIM WRITERS

ASIAN-AMERICAN WRITERS

HISPANIC-AMERICAN WRITERS

NATIVE AMERICAN WRITERS

MULTICULTURAL VOICES

HISPANIC-AMERICAN WRITERS

Union Public Library
1980 Morris Avenue
Union, N.J. 07083

ALLISON AMEND

MULTICULTURAL VOICES: Hispanic-American Writers

Copyright © 2010 by Infobase Publishing

All rights reserved. No part of this book may be reproduced or utilized in any form or by any means, electronic or mechanical, including photocopying, recording, or by any information storage or retrieval systems, without permission in writing from the publisher. For information contact:

Chelsea House
An imprint of Infobase Publishing
132 West 31st Street
New York NY 10001

Library of Congress Cataloging-in-Publication Data
Amend, Allison.
   Hispanic-American writers / Allison Amend.
      p. cm. — (Multicultural voices)
   Includes bibliographical references and index.
   ISBN 978-1-60413-312-7 (hardcover)
   1. Americanliterature—Hispanic-Americanauthors—Historyandcriticism—Juvenile literature. 2. American literature—Hispanic-American authors—Stories, plots, etc—Juvenile literature. 3. American literature—Hispanic-American authors—Themes, motives—Juvenile literature. 4. Hispanic-American authors—Biography—Juvenile literature. 5. Hispanic Americans—Intellectual life—Juvenile literature. 6. Hispanic Americans in literature—Juvenile literature. I. Title. II. Series.
   PS153.H56A64 2010
   810.9'868073—dc22
                                                   2009046535

Chelsea House books are available at special discounts when purchased in bulk quantities for businesses, associations, institutions, or sales promotions. Please call our Special Sales Department in New York at (212) 967-8800 or (800) 322-8755.

You can find Chelsea House on the World Wide Web at
http://www.chelseahouse.com

Series design by Lina Farinella
Cover designed by Alicia Post
Composition by IBT Global, Troy NY
Cover printed by IBT Global, Troy NY
Book printed and bound by IBT Global, Troy NY
Date printed: March 2010
Printed in the United States of America

10 9 8 7 6 5 4 3 2 1

This book is printed on acid-free paper.

All links and Web addresses were checked and verified to be correct at the time of publication. Because of the dynamic nature of the Web, some addresses and links may have changed since publication and may no longer be valid.

CONTENTS

OVERVIEW	7
Rudolfo Anaya	18
Esmeralda Santiago	26
Julia Alvarez	38
Oscar Hijuelos	54
Sandra Cisneros	62
Cristina García	68
Ernesto Quiñonez	78
Junot Díaz	94
CHRONOLOGY	111
ADDITIONAL READING	116
BIBLIOGRAPHY	119
INDEX	122

OVERVIEW

AUTHORS OF HISPANIC DESCENT have contributed to and altered the landscape of contemporary American literature in numerous ways. As part of a recent group of immigrants, coming from a variety of locations throughout the Caribbean and Central and South America, these writers are able to capture the immigrant experience and frame it within a modern lens. Not surprisingly, a central preoccupation in many Hispanic-American literary works, related to the crosscultural realities immigrants face, is the nature of identity. There is no one voice, nor a single vision that can encapsulate or represent the Hispanic-American experience. Instead, regional, national, and language differences contribute to a body of literature as diverse as the individuals producing it.

As a general term, *Hispanic* came to refer to the culture and peoples of the areas once controlled by the Spanish government. The U.S. government first used the designation on the 1970 census, though it was in common and official use before that. As an alternative to Hispanic, *Latino* gained prominence in the 1950s, as people of Central and South American descent wanted to invent a word that differed from the terminology the government imposed. The word is a shortened form of *latinoamericano,* meaning "Latin American." Around the same time, the word *Chicano* also began to circulate. Chicano refers to Americans of Mexican origin, especially those who were part of the area annexed by the United States in the nineteenth century, including California, Texas, and New Mexico.

Chicano literature is just one thread or subset of Hispanic-American writing. Another significant presence is Nuyorican literature, or literature by people of Puerto Rican descent. Cuban literature has also emerged, with its own defined historical and political concerns, much of it produced by those in exile after Fidel Castro seized control of the island in February 1959. Finally, a group of writers that has recently added its voice to the growing body of Hispanic-American literature are those who trace their origins to the Dominican Republic. These authors often address or explore the lingering wounds inflicted by the regime of Rafael Trujillo.

These authors, immigrants or the descendants of immigrants, write in English, a language they either grew up speaking or adopted. Often, in their works, writers employ Spanglish, a hybrid or mixed form of Spanish and English commonly spoken in bilingual households. Spanish phrases or Spanish terms for which there are no suitable English equivalents are commonly incorporated.

The forging of this new language—and its appearance on the printed page and in published works—is a symbol and manifestation of the pride Hispanic-American authors take in their culture. It is also a mark of distinction that sets these literary works apart. The struggle to assimilate or blend into American life, while maintaining traditional values and customs, is frequently depicted and dramatized in the works. Criticism is not suspended or withheld, even within a celebration of cultural pride and vitality. Authors examine the beliefs and attitudes that have long informed their cultures, just as they may question the superstition, criminality, sexism, and racism they see in their communities. Most of all, these authors give voice to a segment of the population that once had little chance to express itself in literature. When Junot Díaz won the Pulitzer Prize for Fiction in 2008, the award only confirmed that Hispanic writing has left a permanent mark on the expanding and ever-changing American literary canon.

Regional Histories

Hispanic-American authors often write about characters who have immigrated in order to flee political persecution or economic hardship. Because of this central concern, it is crucial that those who study the key works know some of the political history that informs these writings. Fictionalized portraits of actual political figures and historical events lend the works authority and complexity, influencing the plots and the course of the protagonists' lives. While historical and political concerns are not always a central influence in the authors' works, the legacy of the past—especially in the form of discrimination, inequality, and political violence—is often seen as hard to escape and impossible to forget.

Mexico

Mexico was occupied up until the sixteenth century by native civilizations of Mesoamerica, including, first, the various ethnic groups that made up the ancient Mayan civilization and then the Aztecs, who were in power when Spanish explorers arrived in 1519. These conquistadores, or conquerors, quickly subdued the population with their horses and firearms. Additionally, the diseases, including smallpox, they brought with them and to which the native population had no immunity caused widespread death.

The Spanish ruled with an iron fist, imposing Catholicism and outlawing many native customs. New Spain became the largest provider of resources for the Spanish empire, as well as its most populated colony. There was much intermarriage, and a strict caste system emerged that created a hierarchy based on race. The Spanish remained in power until 1810 when Mexico declared its independence. It was not until nearly 11 years later, however, that the Mexican people finally overthrew the Spanish colonizers.

A tumultuous period followed, marked by a string of varying government administrations, until 1876 when Porfirio Díaz won the first of five presidential elections. The last, in 1910, was marred by accusations of fraud and instigated the Mexican Revolution, resulting in the constitution of 1917.

Slowly, through the nineteenth century, Mexican holdings were reduced as tracts of land were lost or ceded to the United States. Texas declared itself an independent republic in 1836 and was officially annexed by the United States in 1845. The Mexican Cession, the result of the Mexican-American War, brought present-day California, Nevada, and Utah and portions of Wyoming, Colorado, New Mexico, and Arizona in 1848. The Gadsden Purchase in 1853 transferred control of the remaining southern portions of New Mexico and Arizona to the United States. During each of these transfers of territorial control, residents had the choice of becoming U.S. citizens, and most opted to, believing that the U.S. government was able to prevent Indian raids and secure a brighter economic future for them.

Some Mexicans were naturalized citizens when their territories became states; others came to work on the railroads or participate in the gold rush. Still others were (and still are) migrant laborers. By the mid-twentieth century, organizations and individuals advocated for Chicano rights and helped to establish a more visible Chicano identity and presence throughout the Southwest and across the United States. Literature was one of the driving forces for this greater exposure and integration. The history of U.S. and Mexican relations is one of shifting and redrawn borders. This concern weighs heavily on the works of many Mexican-American writers who examine, similarly, the shifting borders of identity, community, awareness, and acceptance.

The Dominican Republic

The Caribbean island now known as the Dominican Republic was occupied and controlled by the Taino ethnic group until Christopher Columbus landed there in 1492 and declared the region Spanish property, naming it *la Espanola*. The capital was established in 1496 and became the first permanent European settlement in the New World. Within one hundred years, the Taino population was nearly eliminated, though traces survive in the racial and ethnic heritage of many Dominicans. Once Spain established its hold in Mexico (New Spain), the empire lost interest in the small island and ceded it to France in 1697. The colony became a center of agriculture, powered mostly by slave labor imported from Africa. A series of revolutions ensued, led alternately by European-born islanders, slaves, and those sympathetic to both the Spanish and French causes. By the mid-1800s, the western part of the island had established its independence as Haiti. The eastern half would waver between Spanish, Haitian, and independent control until 1863, when it established itself as a country. A long period of government upheavals, violent revolutions, and assassinations plagued the nation. U.S. president Theodore Roosevelt, interested in Dominican affairs primarily to protect American investment in the Panama Canal, ordered troops to occupy the nation from 1916 to 1922.

The violence and instability that marked the nation's early years extended into the reign of dictator Rafael Leonidas Trujillo Molina, who ruled the country through fear, coercion, and torture. While he helped improve the nation's health care, education, and infrastructure and eliminated the country's massive debt, these contributions do not overshadow the devastation he inflicted. He ordered the massacre of all Haitians living in the Dominican Republic, as determined by their skin color, though he himself was part Haitian and up to 70 percent of Dominicans self-identify as biracial or of mixed race. Families were required to hang portraits of the dictator in their homes or be subjected to incarceration by the secret police, the SIM. Trujillo routinely quashed any attempts at revolution or dissent, including murdering the three Mirabal sisters who were working to overthrow him (as related in Julia Alvarez's fictionalized account *In the Time of the Butterflies*). His self-obsession resulted in his renaming major cities, sites, and districts after him and his family. Intellectual Dominicans fled the island, while U.S. officials determined that Trujillo, a sympathizer with the American government, was better than an unknown elected official. Trujillo's reign of terror, lasting from 1930 to 1961, ended with his assassination.

Subsequent regimes were still brutal, supported by the United States in order to prevent pro-Castro forces from overrunning the country. The modern government is an elected democracy, but Trujillo's legacy of economic disparity and violence still scars the nation and influences the Dominican literary voices that have emerged in recent years.

Cuba

Cuba's history shares certain parallels with the history of the Dominican Republic. Located in the Caribbean Sea, Cuba is a series of islands that was also claimed by Spain in 1492. It remained under Spanish rule until 1898, exporting its valuable supplies of sugar, coffee, and tobacco. The United States tried repeatedly to buy or annex the island and, in 1898, gained control of Cuba as a result of the Spanish-American War. From 1902—the year of its independence—until the 1950s, the country was led by a series of various leaders and governments. Following a long struggle for power, Fidel Castro became prime minister (and later president) in February 1959, a post he held for almost 50 years.

Castro, a staunch communist, seized control of all major Cuban industries and businesses. As tensions between U.S. president John F. Kennedy and Castro heightened in the 1960s, culminating with the Cuban Missile Crisis of 1962, Cuba forged closer ties to the Soviet Union, receiving aid and supplies from that country and sending troops in support of Soviet military actions in Ethiopia, Angola, and Afghanistan. When the Soviet Union was dissolved in 1991, Cuba ceased to receive the financial aid it had grown to depend on and faced strict U.S. sanctions. Since the revolution of 1959, more than 2 million Cubans have left the island. A second wave of immigration occurred in 1980, when Castro temporarily lifted the emigration embargo and people fled to countries they felt were more supportive of human rights, personal freedom, and economic opportunity. Cuban-American writers have come to view their native nation and their exile through various perspectives. Cuba appears in various guises, as a mythical place haunting individual and collective memory as well as a forbidden land Cuban immigrants never knew or will never have access to again.

Puerto Rico

Puerto Rico began as a Taino settlement conquered by Christopher Columbus. Despite several failed attempts at gaining independence, it remained a colony of Spain, until the United States invaded as part of the Spanish-American War of 1898. Puerto Rico then became a U.S. territory, a status that granted it various degrees of autonomy. In 1947, the United States granted Puerto Rico the right to elect its own governor; in 1952, the people voted by referendum to declare the nation a commonwealth. Puerto Ricans are U.S. citizens and may vote in the island's elections but not in federal ones, even though the U.S. president is their head of state.

This evolving identity, political status, and relationship to the United States has deeply informed and influenced literature produced by Americans of Puerto Rican descent. Many works explore the nature of what it means to be Puerto Rican and if and how that definition changes when borders are crossed. The tensions between urban and rural and the distinctions of class and economic mobility yield additional complexity to the novels and memoirs inspired by the island's history and life.

Literary History

Though Latin American immigrants in the United States had always written and produced literary works, when the civil rights movement gained momentum in the 1960s, Hispanic-produced literature surged in prominence. Many writers found the various literary genres they employed the ideal means of giving voice to the discrimination or silence they felt imposed on them through racism, poverty, and governmental oppression.

One of the first Hispanic-American literary movements emerged from the Chicano Renaissance, which began nearly simultaneously in California with the founding of the Teatro Campesino (Farm Workers Theater) and in Texas with the publication of the pioneering poetry collection *25 Pieces of a Chicano Mind* by Abelardo Delgado. Following the success of this work, other poets and writers, mostly working class and self-taught, began to publish in literary journals (*Caracol*—meaning "snail"—and *Tejidos* were the best known). In 1971, Tomás Rivera published *Y no se lo tragó la tierra* (. . . *And the Earth Did Not Part*), which was awarded a prize from Quinto Sol Publications, a California-based Mexican-American publishing house. Other authors such as Rolando Hinojosa-Smith won international recognition, and Texas became a major center of Chicano literature, with festivals, publishing houses, and an established community of writers. Though the movement began to taper off after about 10 years, its groundbreaking acceleration served as a model for other national literary movements.

In New York, Puerto Rican authors were experiencing a similar awakening. Piri Thomas wrote *Down These Mean Streets* in 1967, a coming-of-age novel that highlighted his experiences with drugs, gangs, violence, and racism. The work helped give rise to a style called "Mean Streets," which traditionally follows Puerto Rican protagonists as they grow from boys to men. At the same time, poet Miguel Algarin emerged as a powerful influence on Puerto Rican literature. In his living room in New York City's East Village, he held court with many of the writers from his Nuyorican Poetry anthology, including Miguel Piñero, whose play *Short Eyes* had received several awards. By 1980, the salon had outgrown both the living room and its new home at a bar, and the Nuyorican Poets Café purchased a building on East 3rd Street in Manhattan where it continues to host and sponsor arts events, giving a stage to underrepresented and emerging voices in American music, literature, and drama.

Common Themes

Though the literatures that sprang from these various countries are obviously different and defined on their own terms, common themes emerge and unify the works of the diverse voices producing them. A central theme centers on the immigrant experience. Many of the protagonists in the works of Hispanic-American authors come from privileged or educated backgrounds that mean little to nothing in their new country. Even if the characters' origins are meager, most find assimilation into American life difficult. With few exceptions, the immigrants stay within a neighborhood of people from their country of origin and know few "Americans." Those they do know are often racist, yelling epithets like "spic" and telling them to return home.

This reception results in an ambiguous or unresolved sense of identity. A lack of acceptance or the overt expression of racism causes feelings of alienation in the characters. They are not welcome in their new society, but they do not entirely or any longer fit in with those whom they left behind. They are no longer Cuban or Mexican or Dominican or Puerto Rican but rather an often confusing blend of the two. The immigrant experience is not always fraught with struggle and challenge, but the sense of transition, of geographic and linguistic change, looms over many of the works these authors produce.

This hybridization or mixture of cultural influences is symbolized by the use of Spanglish. The authors often use Spanish phrases or words without offering an English translation. The non-Spanish speaker can often, but not always, glean the meaning from the context. Spanglish performs two key functions. First, it gives the reader a representation of actual verbal patterns and exchanges, of language as it is used and adapted. The use of Spanish highlights the interplay of the two languages, their fluid natures, as immigrants learn English words or convert new concepts into their native tongue. Second, the non-Spanish-speaking reader feels the same sense of isolation and alienation many immigrant populations experience, the sensation of being shut out of the narrative because of the barriers of language and communication. In effect, the reader becomes an immigrant in the world of the story.

Most of the works examined in this volume take up, at least in part, the challenges of learning a new language, the insecurities and vulnerabilities that can result as immigrants struggle or fail to communicate. Younger characters become the victims of merciless teasing or are unable to express their talents or intelligence at school due to their lack of English.

Achieving fluency then potentially presents another set of concerns. Once the young person has become accustomed to speaking English, he or she is sometimes reluctant to speak Spanish with the older generation, causing a rift between parents and children that becomes symbolic of the disagreements and growing cultural divide that separates them. The older generation is often and unrightly portrayed as old-fashioned or stuck in the past, while the young feel like they are forging new paths and making greater strides toward assimilation. Children are embarrassed that their parents do not speak English or that they have an accent. Additionally, children are occasionally forced to take on the role of parent, explaining how things work in the United States or translating for officials. The gap between those who acquire English fluency and those who refuse or are unable to is yet another reality influencing the work of Hispanic-American writers.

One legacy of immigration is often poverty, and the crushing lack of resources that the majority of these characters feel is prominently displayed. Readers are confronted with families that have no money for clothes, much less proper nutrition or school supplies. Privacy is a major concern as well, as families are crammed into small apartments. Additionally, poverty forces many of the characters to forgo education in order to contribute to the family's financial livelihood.

Therefore, any opportunity for advancement in society is hindered by the pressure to make enough money and the essential need to survive.

Violence is another common theme in these works. Political violence touches the history of many of the countries to which the writers trace their origins. For some immigrants, it is precisely this violence that they are fleeing, only to find it in their own neighborhoods and lives. Gangs and violent crime abound. Police officers are frequently portrayed as insensitive or failing to understand the cultural circumstances surrounding the crimes.

Violence also occurs within families. Many of the stories include examples of violence against women. Codes of male dominance and male power are transferred to the individuals' new communities and homes. Frustration, poverty, and a sense of a lack of power spill over into physical confrontation or undisguised infidelity. For many women, traditional roles become radically redefined, as many female characters are forced to seek work outside the home, with no reduction or alteration to the domestic chores and tasks they are still expected to perform.

In the wake of this sexism, a feminist movement breaks through. Despite often rigidly enforced social codes, many of the female characters are able to buck these restrictive gender roles and achieve a greater sense of personal and often sexual power. One way is through education; acquiring knowledge is seen as one way of making themselves independent of male dominance. These transitions and growing awareness are often cast within the framework of the traditional coming-of-age tale, as the child grows and learns to confront and navigate the responsibilities and moral complexities of the adult world. Part of this maturation process is recognizing the harsh realities that exist and influence life in their communities and neighborhoods. Another aspect of growing up comes in figuring out how to respect the customs and expectations of the family, while still absorbing and fitting into the new American culture.

Rebellion, thus, is another common theme. Parents are frequently portrayed as strict and controlling. Many hover over their children, stifling their growing independence. Yet, it is the portrayal of the gradual loosening or breaking down of these standards that give these works much of their power. Religion often hovers in the background of these works as a strong influence, regulating conduct and demanding the appearance of a regulated and moral life. The Catholic religion, forced on native populations by the Spanish colonizers, has merged in some cases with native African and indigenous Central American beliefs to form a highly influential belief system. Church attendance is almost always mandatory, and parents often pray to saints as though they were gods, creating altars and looking for divine signs. The children nearly uniformly reject this spirituality, considering it outdated and representative of an older order.

Members of the younger generation are also portrayed as starting to question their parents' devotion to Christianity. Some characters see their parents as hypocritical, demanding a piety they are unable to achieve in their own lives. There is a fascination with Santería (a religion blending West African and Roman Catholic influences) as a way of getting in touch with the native roots of people from the Caribbean rim. Additionally, indigenous religions, mixed with West African belief systems and Catholicism have give rise to a hybrid religion that is attractive to young people precisely because it straddles various worlds and cultural influences, just as they do.

Within this context of moral conduct and intergenerational struggle, family emerges as a topic of paramount importance. Many of the books include family trees as part of their introductions, and many of the works are multigenerational epics. Readers often get to know, or need to know, the history and interconnections of a broad cast of characters. Often, geography—in addition to language and evolving attitudes—separates family members, with grandparents, aunts, and uncles not making the move to the United States.

The strength and influence of family is also evident in the custom of keeping the mother's last name in addition to the father's. It is a way of honoring and remembering both sides of the family tree. It is this bond, also, that reinforces the close ties between mothers and children and explains why so many of the characters feel they need to protect, improve, or heal relationships with their families.

Hispanic-American literature is a literature of escape. Immigrants have escaped their homelands; children struggle to escape their parents' rules and interference in their lives. Often, children fight to escape the stigma of foreignness, of racism, and of feeling like they belong neither in the United States nor in their home countries. Fear, too, infects many of the families. They fear being evicted, deported, or shunned by the community.

Skin color emerges as a significant concern in these works as well. The legacy of the Spanish caste system created social attitudes and a hierarchy that for some is difficult to overcome. The lighter your skin, the more elevated and sophisticated you may seem. Immigrants who considered themselves of an elevated status in their home country are shocked to find themselves in a United States that considers them second-class citizens—exotic or inferior.

Despite common themes and shared concerns and preoccupations, there are regional differences informing and distinguishing the various strands and traditions that collectively make up Hispanic-American literature. Puerto Rican literature is typically more focused on the intricacies of Spanglish, since many of the immigrants arrive speaking English already. Dominican and Cuban literature tends to be more concerned with politics, since most of the emigrants from those nations left as a direct result of the oppressive political regimes. Chicano literature often explores the degradations of poverty, while Puerto Rican literature commonly addresses the latent racism within American society. Because they are citizens, Puerto Ricans do not have the same immigration and visa issues as others; they feel, though, that they should be accepted by a society often unwilling or slow to recognize them as U.S. citizens.

Chicano and Nuyorican literature comes out of a civil rights movement that is still alive today. From the Mexican labor boycotts of the 1960s to the activist Young Lords in Harlem, these two traditions stem from an engagement in the struggle for acceptance and equality and a tradition of protest and dissent. In their works, the authors affirm their commitment to voicing their opinions and gaining equal rights.

Although there is a wealth of voices, concerns, and viewpoints represented in contemporary Hispanic-American literature, overall it reflects a diverse community that has banded together around a similar heritage, similar customs, and a similar language to forge a vehicle for expression that had not yet been previously established or available. The works can thus take on an experimental tone, using poetry and vignettes (based on the strong oral tradition in Latin America) and the fantastical qualities of magical realism to relate their stories. If these authors' individual experiences and stories are new to the American scene, if they are breaking new literary ground and offering and injecting their voices where once there was silence, contemporary Hispanic-American writers have adapted traditional approaches as well as developed new literary tools and forms in order to do so.

RUDOLFO ANAYA

Biography

RUDOLFO ANAYA'S WORK is often autobiographical, so it is no surprise that he shares many characteristics of the main character, Antonio, in his award-winning work *Bless Me, Ultima*. Anaya was born in Pastura, New Mexico, on October 30, 1937. His father, a cowboy working on the plains, was his mother's second husband; Anaya had six siblings and three half siblings. As in his novel, his mother was the daughter of farmers. His father's ancestors included one of the original developers of the New Mexican land grant.

The family moved soon after Anaya's birth to Santa Rosa. Anaya's memories of his post–World War II childhood are idyllic; racism and discrimination were almost nonexistent, and he felt secure in his faith as a student of Catholicism. When the family moved to Albuquerque when Anaya entered high school, however, he began to see his native New Mexico in a different light. While living in a suburb, Anaya was exposed to the poverty faced by many of the Chicanos who had moved to the city in search of opportunity. He saw that his neighborhood was full of gangs and drugs. Twice in his life, Anaya escaped death. First, a *curadera*, a traditional female practitioner of folk medicine, much like the one he describes in his novel, was able to untangle the umbilical cord from around his neck at birth. Then, in high school, he fractured two vertebrae diving into water. He was in the hospital for months and then paralyzed for several more before recovering fully. During that time, he read many books and began to wonder if he had been saved for a reason.

He enrolled in business school after graduating high school in 1956 but quickly realized it was not the path for him. He attended the University of New Mexico, working his way through as a bookkeeper. The experience was scarring. "We were Mexican students," he recalls, "unprepared by high school to compete as scholars. We were tolerated rather than accepted. The thought was still prevalent in the world of academia that we were better suited as janitors than scholars." In addition, Anaya's exposure to higher education had shaken his faith—he no longer believed in the Catholic God and sought to replace that sudden absence in his life with a newfound love of writing.

Anaya graduated from the University of New Mexico with an undergraduate degree in English in 1963. He married in 1966, while continuing his studies, receiving a master's degree in 1968. Afterward, he taught school and continued to write in his free time. Anaya received an additional degree in guidance and counseling and worked as a counselor at the University of Albuquerque until the publication of *Bless Me, Ultima* in 1972.

Anaya sought a new voice while writing *Bless Me, Ultima*, a new way of expressing the experience of Chicano people through literature. He looked to a combination of forces that influenced his childhood—the stories of his grandfather, his parents' superstitious beliefs, and a Native American willingness to accept the supernatural—to inform and create a unique style. "I was still imitating a style and mode not indigenous to the people and setting I knew best. I was desperately seeking my natural voice, but the process by which I formed it was long and arduous." He rejected the notion that becoming a good writer was to write like everyone else.

Anaya was deeply affected by the 1960s civil and social protests and the anti–Vietnam War lobby. He became an ardent pacifist, distributing petitions and organizing a teacher's union. Anaya's success was not immediate. He sent his completed novel to many publishers in New York, but all of them rejected it. He also submitted to a contest run by a Chicano press in Berkeley, California, winning the 1971 Quinto Sol Publications Award for the best novel written by a Chicano. *Bless Me, Ultima* went on to become the first Chicano best-seller.

In 1974, Anaya became a professor of literature at the University of New Mexico where he was instrumental in setting up programs for emerging writers and helping to mentor other Chicano authors. He wrote several more works of fiction, essays, and short stories. *Heart of Aztlán* (1976) and *Tortuga* (1979) are considered the "sequels" to *Bless Me, Ultima*. Anaya calls this New Mexico trilogy his fictional autobiography. All three books address coming of age, the effect of war on youth, the cultural heritage of Native Americans, Mexican and Spanish influences, the beautiful New Mexican landscape, and the increasing urbanization of rural areas.

Anaya continued to write prolifically, delving into drama as well as other genres. In 1980, he was invited by President Jimmy Carter to give a reading at the White House and was awarded a fellowship from the Kellogg Foundation, which allowed him to go to China and later publish his journal from his travels there.

Since his retirement in 1993, Anaya has continued to write, embarking on perhaps his most ambitious project to date—The Albuquerque Quartet. This mystery/thriller series takes on drug trafficking, environmentalism, and the vanishing and increasingly compromised New Mexican landscape. He is also working on writing the words to an opera based on the legend of La Llorona. In April 2002,

Anaya was the recipient of the 2001 National Medal of Arts, presented by President George W. Bush at the White House; but it is for *Bless Me, Ultima*, a pioneering work, that he remains best known.

Bless Me, Ultima
Summary and Analysis

Anaya's novel is the history of the New Mexican Chicano experience as told through the eyes of a small boy, Antonio Márez. The novel presents as a matter of course elements of the supernatural that coexist with everyday life. Antonio struggles to grow up and reconcile his conflicted feelings about Catholicism and native beliefs, good and evil, and the changing landscape of his homeland.

The novel begins with an older version of the narrator reminiscing about the time when Ultima (also known as La Grande), a curadera, or healer, came to live out the rest of her days with his family in rural New Mexico. The night before she arrives, Antonio dreams of the night of his birth, when Ultima delivers him from his mother's womb. The ongoing discussion between his parents' respective families hovers in the background. His mother María's side is a family of farmers, rooted and dependent on the soil for their livelihood. His father Gabriel's side is from the plains. They raise cattle and are nomadic and adventurous. Both factions are fighting to control Antonio's destiny.

Antonio awaits Ultima's arrival, worried because school will soon start and he will be away from his mother. When Ultima arrives, Antonio calls her by her given name, Ultima, instead of the term of respect his mother insists on, La Grande. She is not offended; she and Antonio share a connection. Ultima brings her owl with her; though owls are traditionally a sign of evil, the hoots of Ultima's owl are soothing, lulling the family to sleep.

Ultima teaches Antonio about the herbs she uses to cure people and introduces him to the special connection she shares with nature. Then one night Antonio witnesses an event that changes his life. His father, Gabriel, joins a posse to hunt down Lupito, a deranged war veteran. Lupito has killed the sheriff, and on the banks of the river the men debate how to capture him. Gabriel urges the use of reason, not force, but when Lupito draws his gun, the men kill him.

That night, Antonio dreams that he is with his three older brothers, who are off fighting in World War II. They need him to lead them across the river so they can build a castle. A howl sounds: Is it La Llorona, the river witch? Or the soul of Lupito? He draws his priestly tightly around him for protection.

The next morning Antonio goes to church, where he is plagued with doubts. He wonders how his father can take communion after his role in Lupito's death. Antonio is not sure that he wants to be the priest his mother insists he become.

The family travels to El Puerto to help María's family with the harvest. Ultima explains that Antonio's mother's family is like the moon (they are named Luna, the

Spanish word for "moon") while his father's side is like the ever-changing ocean. Ultima also shows him the plants of the plains and explains their importance.

Antonio reluctantly goes to school. His mother reminds him that when he was just a baby and was offered "the objects of life," he chose the pen. It is obvious to her that he will be a scholar. Though he is proud that by the end of the day he learns to write his name, all the other children speak English and laugh at him and his Mexican lunch. He finds a group of boys similar to him, and they stand around the corner of the building during recess, feeling ostracized.

Antonio dreams that his brothers tell him they are coming home. The dream quickly transforms into a nightmare, but when Antonio wakes and runs outside, he sees the figures of his brothers heading home. María is overwhelmed with joy, even though the brothers sleep all day and drink, gamble, and patronize prostitutes at night. After the return of his sons, Gabriel begins to talk again about moving to California, the land of his dreams.

Antonio's brothers tease him about becoming a priest, asking for his blessing then putting him on top of the chicken coop where he cannot get down. Antonio wishes he could have actually blessed them. Later, he dreams again that his brothers invite him to the brothel, but Antonio cannot enter. He has sworn to preserve his innocence forever in order to become a priest. His brothers tell him that because he is half Márez, he will prove to be too wild to ever settle successfully into the priesthood.

Antonio's two oldest brothers leave, upsetting the family. María once again does not have her family intact, while Gabriel will never realize his dream of moving to California. The remaining brother, Andrew, opts for a job at a local grocery. He explains to Antonio that he lost his innocence in the war. Antonio wonders when he will lose his. At school, Antonio learns he will skip second grade and advance to third the following school year. He and his friend Samuel go fishing. Samuel tells him that they should not fish for carp because long ago carp were sacred, but the starving people ate them nonetheless. The gods planned to kill the people for their disobedience, but one god took the people's side. As a punishment, the gods turned the people into fish and the god who was their advocate into a golden carp. Samuel tells the excited Antonio that their friend Cico can show him the golden carp.

Antonio's uncle Lucas has been bewitched. He lies gravely ill after witnessing three "witch" sisters perform their rites. Ultima says she will treat him, but she may unleash events that will be beyond their control if she does. The family tells her to proceed.

Ultima and Antonio go to Tenorio Trementina's bar. He is the father of the three "witch" sisters, and they tell him of their plans to release Lucas from the spell. Ultima and Antonio go to Lucas's side. Antonio assumes Lucas's symptoms. Ultima plans to use Antonio's body to draw the sickness out of Lucas. Antonio writhes and vomits. Ultima creates three clay dolls, sticking pins in each. Lucas then immediately vomits a ball of hair and bile, and Ultima sees that the

Trementina sisters were using his hair to cast a spell on him. Ultima buries the hairball at the site of the rite that Lucas witnessed, and he is cured.

Cico then shows Antonio the golden carp. Antonio is in awe but cannot recognize it as a god because of his Catholic faith. Cico tells his friend the myths surrounding the golden carp and the belief that one day, when too many people have sinned, the golden carp will rule again. Antonio tells Ultima what he saw, but all she says to him is that part of growing up is discovering his own truths.

One of the Trementina sisters dies, and their father, Tenorio, blames Ultima. Antonio's father's friend Narciso warns the family. Tenorio comes to the house, demanding that Ultima appear, but Ultima's owl swoops down and gouges out one of his eyes. Antonio dreams that Ultima is dead, then watches the Trementina funeral procession. Narciso and Tenorio fight over Ultima's supposed witchcraft. Antonio's friend Samuel tells him that this fight will end in bloodshed.

After the Christmas pageant, Tenorio and Narciso fight again in the snow. Narciso goes to the brothel to warn Antonio's brother, but Andrew is not worried. As Narciso then goes to warn Ultima, Tenorio shoots him. Antonio is there to hear Narciso's confession as he dies. That night, Antonio has a terrible dream that he dies without having taken communion and is condemned to Purgatory. An angry mob murders his family and dismembers the body of Ultima. Then the earth falls into a black void, only to be swallowed by the golden carp.

Antonio contracts pneumonia, and while he recuperates, Ultima tells him stories of the old days. He begins preparations for his first communion. Family life is disrupted again with the arrival of police officers, who bring Antonio's two oldest brothers home. They crashed their car and had to burn it for warmth. The next day, all three brothers leave.

Antonio soon becomes obsessed with the nature of good and evil. Specifically, he wonders how God allows evil to take place in the world. He is appalled that no one saw the good in Narciso and that his death went unpunished, while Tenorio is allowed to go free. Antonio begins to pray to the Virgin, whom he thinks may be more understanding.

In March, the U.S. government begins atomic testing, which raises eerie dust storms in the area. Antonio is excited to take his first communion on Easter Sunday, but his enthusiasm is dampened when the other boys tease him and rip off his shirt. He feels certain that God will speak to him during his communion, but he takes the wafer and drinks the wine and hears no voice.

Ultima exorcises demons from a house; it appears that the Trementina sisters have manipulated the ghosts of Comanche Indians to haunt those who are sympathetic to Ultima. There is a rumor that another Trementina sister is close to death. Antonio is confused—Ultima's magic has saved more people than the priest has. He wonders who has more power. His questions are unanswered when he decides to show his atheist friend the golden carp, so he will have evidence at least of one God. The friend, however, drowns in the water before he sees the carp.

Antonio has another apocalyptic nightmare, and Ultima comforts him by saying that it is natural to be sad when changing from a boy into a man. Later, Antonio's father tells him that the age of the untamed plains is over. Antonio must take his wild Márez side and his rooted Luna side and forge a new path built on the scaffolding of the old. Antonio takes this advice to heart, realizing that all of his questions about divinity and good and evil can be reconciled. Gabriel tells his son that Ultima's magic is really just a tremendous sympathy for others.

Another Trementina daughter dies, and Tenorio vows to kill Ultima. Antonio runs toward home but meets Tenorio in the same place where Narciso was shot. Tenorio goes after the boy, but Antonio escapes, hearing Tenorio swear that he will kill Ultima's owl, her protective spirit. Afraid of what will happen to Ultima if her owl dies, Antonio returns home. He is too late; Tenorio kills the owl, after which Antonio's uncle kills Tenorio.

Antonio takes the body of the owl to Ultima, who knows she is dying. She tells Antonio not to worry; she has fulfilled her purpose in life and asserts that she is simply flying away to a new place. Harmony will be restored when both she and Tenorio are dead. She asks Antonio to bury the owl beneath a forked juniper tree. He knows that no matter where Ultima is buried, the tree will be her real resting place.

Antonio's final dream is violent. He rejects the violence and learns that something must die in order for others to live. The figures in his dreams tell him they are just that—inside his dreams. He can stop their visits by fully joining the outside world.

Major Themes
Opposition and Opposing Influences

While many of the works discussed in this volume are set either in New York City or in the immigrants' countries of origin, *Bless Me, Ultima*'s action occurs entirely in New Mexico, near the border with Mexico. The residents travel back and forth across the border and live in communities made up of individuals similar to them. Thus, the idea of assimilation, of blending with a prevailing or dominant culture, so prevalent in other novels, is largely absent here. Though Antonio arrives at school with no English, he is able to learn so quickly that he skips a grade, and he has no trouble making friends. The ideas of assimilation are still embodied, however, in Antonio's struggle to reconcile seeming opposite teachings. The first opposition he confronts exists within his family. His father is a lover of the *llano*, or the barren plains landscape they live among. Yet he dreams of traveling to Mexico to find a better life. Antonio's mother, in contrast, is a Luna and grew up according to the regular natural rhythms of farm life. Her rootedness fights constantly with Gabriel's errant or wandering nature.

Also at odds are the traditional methods of Ultima and the more mainstream Catholicism of Antonio's mother. Ultima believes in the healing power of plants. She is a curadera, a healer who is able to exorcise demons. The rest of the town is not as open-minded when it comes to the old woman's presence. They dismiss

Ultima as a witch. This narrow-mindedness is representative of the entire town, which is unable to accept difference of any kind. Instead of helping Lupito overcome his trauma, they shoot him. The community members are quick to condemn any aberrant behavior.

Meanwhile, Antonio's mother, María, prays fervently. It is her hope that Antonio will be a priest. She is unable to entertain the thought that Antonio will choose his own path. In some ways, the opposition between native religion and Christianity is the same as Antonio's struggle to figure out the difference between good and evil. There are characters who are obviously good in the book, like Ultima, and a few that are portrayed as strictly evil, like Tenorio or La Llorona. The novel's other characters prove hard for Antonio to classify. His brothers are good, though they sin by visiting the brothel. Owls are traditionally a symbol or omen of bad luck, even though, contrary to expectation, Ultima's owl is benevolent. Antonio is also confused by competing divine influences: a God who can be vengeful and the Virgin Mary, who is seen as all-forgiving. Swimming in this mix is the figure of the golden carp, an element from a traditional story that nonetheless seems like a viable candidate for worship.

The Preservation of Innocence

In the face of the struggle to resolve opposing influences, Antonio strives to maintain his innocence. He is determined to remain pure, yet his brothers say that his Márez blood will rise within him and cause him to sin. He is also worried that the violence and evil he has witnessed have stripped him of his innocence. He is unsure if he wants to be a priest but does not want to disappoint his mother. He also wishes that, like Ultima, he had the power to bless and cure. The novel presents the notion that growing up comes at the expense of one's innocense.

Dreams Versus Reality

Dreams appear as episodes in the book. It is clear that Antonio's dreams are prophetic, bearing accurate images of future occurrences. The dreams are also able to influence action in the conscious world. Antonio struggles with the same issues in the realm of sleep and dreams as he does in his waking life. Dreams emerge as symbols of his consciousness, presented in the novel as though they were realistic action. By employing so many dreams, Anaya recalls the storytelling and dream heritage of native practices. The dream sequences also allow the author to dramatize the mental conflict within Antonio.

Nature

A final theme in the novel is the pastoral landscape of New Mexico. Nature is described with a loving and accurate eye. The vast plains, the dry, hot sun, and the dark moon are all characters in this novel of place. When Ultima dies, she tells Antonio to look for her in the evening winds. Death, then, is presented as merely a melding into the landscape.

ESMERALDA SANTIAGO

Biography

ESMERALDA SANTIAGO is a memoirist, novelist, and screenwriter, as well as a frequent contributor to major magazines, journals, and newspapers. Because the two works discussed here are memoirs, much of her biography will be covered in the book synopses. Many details of her life, however, were not included in her writings.

Santiago was born on May 17, 1948, in San Juan, Puerto Rico. As a child, her mother moved the children several times from their small village of Macún to the larger town of Santurce. When Santiago's younger brother Raymond's foot became infected, putting his life in danger, their mother decided to move the children to New York. In her memoirs, Santiago tells the stories of their first years in the city and of her life as the oldest of 11 children. She attended the School of the Performing Arts and eventually graduated (after eight years at various community colleges) from Harvard University in 1976. She married documentary filmmaker Frank Cantor, with whom she has collaborated on many projects, and had two children, who are now both grown.

Santiago did not consider herself a writer, though she contributed essays frequently to many publications. It was not until after the birth of her second child that she took a creative writing class. She was "discovered" by an editor at Perseus Press, who offered her an advance for her life story. Her first memoir, *When I Was Puerto Rican*, was published in 1993, to much acclaim. It focuses on Santiago's earliest years in Puerto Rico and on the displacement she felt at being identified as a hick, an unsophisticated rural dweller, when she moved to Santurce. The book follows the family to New York and traces their first few years as they struggle to survive in the United States.

Santiago took a break between memoirs to write *América's Dream*, a novel, in 1996. Her second memoir, *Almost a Woman*, which retraces some of the same ground as *When I Was Puerto Rican,* follows Santiago through high school and into the beginning of her young adult life, up to the point where she decides to forge her own path. *Almost a Woman* was filmed for television by Exxon Masterpiece Theater's American Collection in 2002. Santiago published her third memoir, *The Turkish Lover,* in 2004.

In between these books, Santiago co-edited an anthology of Hispanic authors' essays on Christmas memories. She followed this book with an anthology of Hispanic authors' tales of their mothers. She also wrote a children's book and various screenplays. In her nonwriting life, Santiago is active in her community in Westchester County, New York. She advocates for public libraries and has founded a shelter for battered women and community programs for teens. In her public speeches, she encourages arts education for young people. She was honored in 2002, alongside Alma Powell and Elizabeth Dole, with a Girl Scouts of America National Woman of Distinction Award.

When I Was Puerto Rican
Summary and Analysis

When I Was Puerto Rican begins with a prologue in which Esmeralda compares a guava purchased from a New York supermarket with one plucked from a tree in Puerto Rico.

The book opens with four-year-old Esmeralda (nicknamed Negi for her dark skin) and her family moving to Macún. Their house is in poor condition. When her father pulls up the floor to replace it, termites attack Negi. It is also located in a rural setting—there are chickens in the yard. Negi sleeps in a hammock, as do her sisters, and is awakened every morning when the rooster crows. Mami gives birth to another child. She is pregnant so frequently that Negi confusedly thinks that her mother's pregnant body is her actual, standard shape.

After Negi's brother Héctor is born, her mother and father begin to fight over money and Papi's other family. Things calm when the other woman and her daughter move to New York City. Negi starts school and learns about a larger world. She also gets into frequent fights. Papi leaves for several days, and Mami takes the children by bus to Santurce, the nearest city, to stay with her extended family.

Mami has another baby, which brings her and Papi closer together. Negi goes to school in the city where she is labeled a *jíbara,* a hick who speaks with a rural accent. Mami agrees to move back to Macún with Papi. When Negi's grandfather dies, it is an opportunity for her father to tell her about life, death, and the soul. Mami has yet another baby. The spring rains come, and she insists that they all take off their clothes and dance in the rain.

It is an election year, and the United States has sent representatives to teach the women about proper nutrition. The women laugh to see the models of toothbrushes. When shown the food pyramid they protest, noting that none of the foods pictured is available in Puerto Rico. They squeal in disgust when told about parasites. Each family is given a bag of groceries courtesy of the U.S. government. Mami puts them away for special occasions.

Negi suffers through a round of vaccinations and a bout of intestinal worms. Then the U.S. government workers start distributing free breakfasts. They are disgusting—powdered eggs, horrible sausages, and prune juice. Negi asks her father how he feels about Americans. He says that some people think they are imperialists. He also tells her not to call them *gringos*, as it is a derogatory term. He reveals the origin of the insult spic (or spik)—from the Hispanic accent when pronouncing the word *speak,* as in "I don't speak English." Negi swears never to become American and to stop learning English in school, but she changes her mind when her grandmother sends her clothes that her cousins have outgrown in New York.

Negi goes to visit her paternal grandparents. Her grandmother takes her to church, where Negi has never been, and teaches her to sew and cook. Her father disappears, and Negi is convinced he has gone to see a woman. She begins to cry, and in order to have another cause for her tears, she slams her hand in the door. When her mother finally comes to comfort her, pregnant again and gushing about the electricity in Negi's grandparents' house, Negi overhears a conversation she is having with Negi's grandmother about her father. Negi swears to remain single, or *jamóna*—an old maid—if being married causes so much emotional pain.

A hurricane hits the island. Macún loses electricity, and the town coffers are depleted. Mami gets a job in the new sewing factory. She is one of few women to work outside the home, and everyone disapproves. Mami says the others are just jealous. With Mami working, Negi, now 10, is in charge of her little brothers and sisters, aided by Gloria, a babysitter. Negi and Tato (a neighbor boy) play "I'll show you mine if you show me yours," but when Tato tries to grab her, she kicks him in the crotch. Her mother beats her severely. She says Negi is "almost señorita" and should no longer be playing with boys.

Gloria tells Negi about menstruation, which scares and unnerves her. Jenny, one of Negi's cousins, is a spoiled only child. Negi is jealous of the attention and toys she receives. When she gets a bicycle, they all want to ride on it, and Negi's youngest brother, Raymond, gets his foot caught in the chain. Everyone blames Jenny, causing Negi to be jealous even of the negative attention her cousin receives. Raymond's foot does not heal and the doctors say he will be physically disabled for life.

Papi grows more distant, and the family moves back to Santurce. They live over a lagoon that gives off a repulsive stench. Once again, Negi is called a jíbara at her school, this time her teacher contributes to the teasing. The city children are more advanced in math, and Negi has trouble keeping up with the rest of the class. When Papi returns, they move again, away from the lagoon to a nicer part of the city but over a noisy bar.

Raymond's foot is still not healed and is badly infected. Papi and Mami fight again, and Papi disappears. Because she has to care for Raymond, she cannot get a job, so she takes in laundry and cooks for the bar. Mami informs Negi that she is going to stay with cousins she has never met. When they get to the cousins' house, Negi discovers that her mother is taking Raymond to New York. She dislikes her cousins—they are mean to her and the family has deeply held evangelical beliefs. Negi is also made to help peel potatoes for the potato balls they sell in their store. She is convinced that her mother is never coming back for her. When she finally returns for her, they get off the bus at the wrong stop. No, Mami says, it is the correct stop. They have moved again.

Mami is told that she can have the morning off if she sends her children to Sunday school, so Negi and her siblings are sent to church, where Negi is delighted by the piano. She wants to learn to play, so, against Mami's wishes, Papi negotiates that the principal of her school will give her lessons in exchange for Papi's carpentry services. During her second lesson, though, the principal tries to look down her blouse, and Negi runs out of his house, calling him a dirty old man. Mami and Papi fight; Mami says she is "casi señorita" or almost a young lady and that the principal should not be trusted.

Mami goes back to New York with Raymond, and the children are left unsupervised. The situation becomes too difficult for Papi to handle, so he takes Negi back to her cousins' house, a punishment. Mami comes to get her, and again Negi is brought to a new home. This time they live next door to a family with a television set, the first the children have been able to watch regularly. Negi gets her own room for the first time. At school, she has a crush on a boy but can only say rude and mean things when he shows interest in her.

Mami comes back from New York with a new purpose. She wants Papi to marry her. They have been together for fourteen years and have seven children, and still he will not marry her and give up his other women. She decides to move to New York. Negi asks if Papi will be joining them, but he says he will never go there. Mami takes the older children and plans to send for the younger ones as soon as she has money. On the airplane, Negi feels as though something has irreparably changed. "The person I was becoming when we left was erased, and another one was created. The Puerto Rican jíbara . . . was to become a hybrid who would never forgive the uprooting."

Arriving in New York, the city is much darker and dirtier than Negi suspected. They move in with Mami's grandmother, Tata, in a small apartment. At school, the principal tries to put Negi in the seventh grade, but she convinces him that she belongs in the eighth grade, even though she barely speaks any English at all. They put her in the class with disruptive and misbehaving students, but still Negi learns. She visits the library daily, and by Christmas speaks enough to achieve high scores on her exams. She learns the hierarchy of her school. The children segregate themselves into ethnic groups, and Negi learns about Jews and Italians. There is a division, she notes, between Puerto Ricans born in the United States and those born in Puerto Rico. Among the immigrants there is an additional divide between those who miss the island and those who want to assimilate into American society. Negi is not sure where she stands in the spectrum.

Mami falls in love with a man—Francisco—10 years her junior, and she and Tata fight about whether or not it is appropriate for Mami to have such a young boyfriend. Tata drinks excessively, and Mami moves the family, which now includes the rest of the children, to another apartment. Francisco moves in. Negi begins to menstruate; she is finally a señorita, not an "almost woman." Her mother brings her a bra home from the factory where she works. It is so cold in Brooklyn that they use the open oven for heat.

Soon after Mami and Francisco's baby is born—a boy also named Francisco, called Franky—Francisco is diagnosed with cancer and dies soon afterward. Mami is inconsolable. Soon, she is laid off from her job. She pulls Negi out of school to translate for her at the welfare office. When Negi comes home late from the library, her mother flies into a rage. Negi dares her to hit her, but Mami does not. Negi is growing up. She hides her makeup from her mother and lets boys walk her home.

At school, the guidance counselor asks Negi what she wants to do when she grows up. He sees that she is intelligent and wants to send her to an academic high school. Negi does not want to become a scientist or educator. She thinks about the Miss America pageant she saw on television and tells the counselor she wants to be a model. He decides she means actress and helps her audition for the School of Performing Arts. What Negi really wants, though, is to return to Puerto Rico. She misses grass and open spaces. Her mother asks if she also misses no electricity and having to use the outhouse.

Many of the school's teachers band together to help Negi prepare for her audition. Mami buys her a new dress for the occasion and even lets her wear a bit of lipstick. Negi is so nervous that her monologue is unintelligible, and she flubs the questions. The judges ask her to come back in and pantomime decorating a Christmas tree. Negi has never had a Christmas tree but performs the scene anyway. In the hallway, she sees a bulletin board with the names, photos, and dates of graduation of famous alumni. She feels sure she has failed the audition and will never see her name on the board.

In an epilogue, an adult Esmeralda, now on full scholarship to Harvard, returns to the School of Performing Arts, which not only admitted her but from which she graduated. Her mentor tells her how funny they all found her audition, but that her spunk impressed them. It took a lot of courage, she says, for Negi to stand up in front of them and recite her monologue. She also reminds Negi how embarrassed she was to have her mentor find out that Negi had to accompany her mother to the welfare office. The mentor comforted her, telling her that many students in the school received assistance. Negi thanks her for her help, and the mentor says how proud she is at how far Negi has come. As Negi walks out of the school, she sees the bulletin board and thinks, someday.

Major Themes

Growing Up in Two Worlds

When I Was Puerto Rican is a love letter to the author's island. Though Santiago grew up in a household plagued by strife and poverty, the island itself is always described glowingly, in ornate prose that brings the beauty of the place alive.

The most traumatic event in Negi's life is without a doubt her move to New York, but even before relocating, the United States exists as a source of anxiety for Negi. She resents American interference and the attempt to influence, if not control, island life. Americans, she believes, are out of touch; they lack the food and resources found in Puerto Rico. They are imperialistic, and Negi resents the implication that her parents need help caring for her. The American-supplied breakfasts make her sick. Negi worries every time Mami goes to New York that she will not come back.

To balance these sentiments, Santiago concedes the positive aspects of the United States. It is a source of beautiful clothes. It is where Raymond goes to get his foot cared for. These two worlds and divisive influences compete in Negi's young mind. When the family permanently moves to New York, Negi recognizes the moment as one that changes not only her life but her identity, her sense of who she is, forever. First, they are leaving behind their father. She knows that she will never live with him again and worries that he will forget about her. Just as impactful is Negi's separation from her native country. She realizes that she is leaving Puerto Rico behind and feels she will never again be able to identify herself as Puerto Rican.

Coming of Age

Tied in with these competing cultural and geographic influences is the confusion Negi expresses about love and adulthood. To her, adulthood is about things she cannot do. As an "almost señorita," she cannot play with boys, walk alone, and has to sit a certain way. The examples of romantic relationships she sees are her parents, unmarried, who fight as violently and passionately as they make up. Theirs is not a stable union. Whenever there is a major disagreement, either Papi or Mami leaves, often deliberately staying out of touch. Negi is as confused and concerned about the times they make up as the times they fight.

The unstable parental relationship leaves the family unsettled and consistently on the move. Negi becomes adept at packing her few belongings and taking a bus to her new home. She rarely has enough time to become accustomed to walking to school before she is transferred to a new one. The biggest transition for her, however, is from country to city life, where she is behind in math and is called jíbara or "hick." This is not so different from the taunting she is subjected to at her school in the Untied States, where she is called "spik" and is behind because of her lack of English.

Negi is, therefore, never able to put down roots. She considers herself from the island of Puerto Rico rather than from a particular town or neighborhood. Her parents often leave her with relatives she does not know, which in some ways prepares her for the nomadic life that Mami subjects the family to in New York. Still, in other ways, Negi will always long for stability.

Mami's ambition is one of the main reasons the family moves so much. Mami is continually looking for a better home, a better position, and greater opportunities. Therefore, she takes a job at a sewing factory at a time when few women work outside the home. She returns from her visits to New York with renewed vigor, excited to be starting a new life where there is better opportunity. Negi inherits this ambition. It is what makes her fight to stay at grade level, what pushes her to audition for the School for the Performing Arts, and, later, what gets her a scholarship to Harvard University.

Almost a Woman
Summary and Analysis

In 1961, Esmeralda Santiago leaves Macún, Puerto Rico, for New York City. During the next eight years, she moves many more times, each time packing her bags with renewed hope for the future. The memoir follows Negi, as she is called, from her early teenage years, trapped in a small apartment with her many siblings, her strict mother, and her grandmother to young adulthood, when she sneaks out on a series of disastrous dates and starts to forge a path for herself in a world that is not quite Puerto Rican, not quite American.

It is hope that first brings the Santiago clan, Mami and her seven children, to New York, to seek medical help for Negi's youngest brother. When Esmeralda first arrives in Brooklyn, she is forced to attend a special-education class because of her lack of English. Though she manages to make a friend, her mother practically forbids her to spend any time outside the apartment, though the quarters are cramped, with two to three children per bed. Just when Negi begins to get accustomed to her new life (but not Americanized: "a terrible thing to be avoided at all costs," according to Mami), her mother loses her job and brings Esmeralda to the welfare office to act as a translator. Their apartment is filled with roaches and is unheated. It appears that life in the United States is not the haven Esmeralda had hoped for.

Instead of finding stability and happiness, Negi lies in her shared bed at night dreaming of her estranged father, fantasizing that he will win back their mother's love and the family will be reunited in Puerto Rico. When a letter arrives announcing that her father has married, her disappointment is immense, as "with Papi married, our ties to Puerto Rico unraveled," the island growing more and more idyllic and distant in her memories.

Mami's pregnancy startles no one, and the family moves in with Don Francisco. Just after his son is born, however, he becomes terminally ill. Again the family goes to the welfare office; this time Esmeralda is better prepared. Her English has improved so much that her guidance counselor recommends she attend a college preparatory school. Esmeralda applies to the Performing Arts High School in Manhattan. Though Mami buys her a new dress and allows her to wear stockings to the audition, it is clear that she greets Esmeralda's Americanization with mixed feelings. "[S]he said . . . that I thought I deserved more and was better than everyone else, better than her. She looked at me resentfully."

Esmeralda is surprised that she gets into the selective school, even though she feels she flubbed the audition. The teasing and name-calling she endures there escalate into a beating. Esmeralda is constantly made aware of her identity as an outsider, a "Latina," "Hispanic," or even sometimes a "spic."

High school brings new challenges, as Esmeralda must now ride the subway to and from Manhattan each morning. The deserted early-morning streets scare her, and men take advantage of the crowded trains to press up against her and expose themselves. At school, she works hard to eradicate all traces of her Puerto Rican and Brooklyn accents and receives training in drama, dance, and theatrical makeup. She feels ashamed that she has failed geometry and must make it up in summer school.

Mami gradually emerges from her mourning of Don Francisco and takes Negi to a nightclub where she learns that she loves to dance. She and her sisters go dancing nearly every weekend after that. At 16, it is Esmeralda's first experiences with men, dancing close during slow numbers, and she struggles with her emerging feelings. She also begins to realize that Mami's strict rules seem to apply only to her children. "We never went to church, but I should marry in a cathedral. A good girl, I should not be too good or my goodness was suspect. If I was too anxious to leave home, my life could turn to tragedy. If I lingered under Mami's protection, I was sure to be deceived by those more knowledgeable in the ways of the world."

Esmeralda's junior year in high school finds her succeeding, finally passing geometry, being cast several times as Cleopatra due to her "exotic" looks, and finding a job as an usher in a Yiddish theater that provides her some spending money. Though she was never particularly gifted in dance, she wins a role as an Indian classical dancer in a children's play.

By the time Esmeralda graduates, Mami has two more children with her married partner, Don Carlos. Though encouraged to go to college, Esmeralda decides to enter the workforce, getting a job as a typist. Her neighbor, Neftalí, begins to court her in a way that Mami approves: He comes over for group dinners and to play cards. When he is drafted, though, Esmeralda is not sad. She goes on her first date, with a Jewish man from the office, and then begins to date other men. She takes advantage of her company's benefits to enroll in community college where she meets Shoshana, a spunky Israeli girl who quickly becomes her best friend and cohort.

Esmeralda is cast in a children's play that will be performed on Broadway and then tour the East Coast. In each town, she feels the stares as she is typically the only nonwhite person, but back in New York, her appearance is more commonly a source of intrigue. Men approach her on the street, and she has a series of relationships. Her partners buy her dresses, take her to dinner, give her presents, but each ultimately disappoints her. Avery Lee, a visiting Texan, tells her he loves her but cannot marry her because "it wouldn't look right for me to have a Spanish wife." Still, he invites her to be his mistress: "I'll get you an apartment, a car, whatever you need." When Otto, an enormous German man who works with her, takes her to his sister's house on Long Island for a Christmas party, Mami and Don Carlos grow suspicious and borrow a car, crashing the party and mortifying Negi. Jurgen, a German with a criminal past also shows romantic interest in Negi. Another suitor proposes, but even though her family makes arrangements for the wedding, Esmeralda calls it off; they barely know each other.

Esmeralda then meets Ulvi Dogan, a Turkish film director who professes he wants nothing to do with her life. While over the course of several months they grow closer, still he remains distant; when she breaks a date to see a friend in a play, his anger surprises her. Then, just as she has suspected, one day he tells her he must leave. He asks her to come with him, but Esmeralda immediately balks—her mother would never allow it. "You must leave her, then," he says, but Esmeralda realizes that she cannot leave her mother.

> He hadn't been there ... hadn't heard the pain in her voice when she mourned her unfinished education, young unmarried motherhood, men who betrayed her. He hadn't been with her at the welfare office, had not stood solemn and scared as she humbled herself before people who would conquer her pride because they couldn't vanquish her spirit. He'd never placed his head on her lap, had never listened as she revealed her dreams for her children, who would, she hoped, be smarter about life than she had been.

As she returns home to her chaotic family, to the bed she still shares with her sister, she concludes that she has made the right choice.

Major Themes

This coming-of-age story shares several of the themes common to many works by Hispanic authors. The pull of assimilation and the simultaneous magnetism that the "old country" holds are especially strong in this memoir, as Negi's memories of Puerto Rico are sweetened by nostalgia for her father and homeland, along with her anger at his betrayal of her family.

Language and Bilingualism

The memoir highlights the dichotomy between the two languages. Negi's first experience with English puts her in a class for misbehaving and mentally challenged children. Then she is forced, to her shame, to translate for her mother at the welfare office. She spends hours practicing speaking, attempting to eradicate not only the Spanish inflections but also the Brooklyn accent that betray her upbringing.

Nearly all her relationships are with immigrants—Israelis, Germans, Turks, Indians—people for whom English is as foreign as it remains to her, even as she speaks it fluently.

Movement/Relocation

Moving is a constant theme in *Almost a Woman*. The book opens with the line, "In the twenty-one years I lived with my mother, we moved at least twenty times." These moves are both metaphoric and literal. Each time, the family tries to move up the ladder of society—looking for a home that is bigger, cleaner, safer than the one before. Negi's lack of privacy plagues her; in almost all the lodgings she shares a bed with at least one of her 10 siblings. Cockroach infestations and a lack of heat and security serve to remind her of their poverty and the sense of alientation it deepened. On the trip each day into Manhattan, "the skyline . . . receded like an enormous wall between us and the rest of the United States."

Cultural Assimilation

One way the theme of assimilation is presented in the book is through food. American food is contrasted with the superior produce of Puerto Rico. Negi and her siblings want to assimilate into American culture by consuming American food—prepackaged cookies, pizza, and soda—while her mother is convinced that Puerto Rican food is better for them. The staples Mami is used to feeding her family—rice, beans, and powdered milk—are also less expensive and can be bought in bulk. The children develop a fetish for American junk food, as a symbol of their assimilation into American society.

Transitions of the Teen Years

The memoir also focuses on the thin line between childhood and adulthood. Negi gradually comes to understand that the adults in her life are flawed. Some are hypocritical, while others do not understand as much as they think they do. She negotiates the in-between world of the teenager, forced to live under her mother's rules but also treated as a woman by the larger world. She chafes at Mami's strict control, even as Mami herself does not aspire to live by these rules. "My world was dominated by adults, their rules written in stone, in Spanish, in Puerto Rico. In my world, no allowance was made for the fact that we were now in the United States, that our language was becoming English, that we were foreigners awash in American culture."

She longs, like many teenagers, to be elsewhere. "I wanted to live in those uncrowded, horizontal landscapes, painted in primary colors . . . where teenagers like me lived in blissful ignorance of violence and grime, where no one had seven sisters and brothers, where grandmothers didn't drink beer late into the night and mothers didn't need you to translate for them at the welfare office." In short, Negi wants to make a better life for herself, and it is this resolve that drives her to attend school and then work in Manhattan.

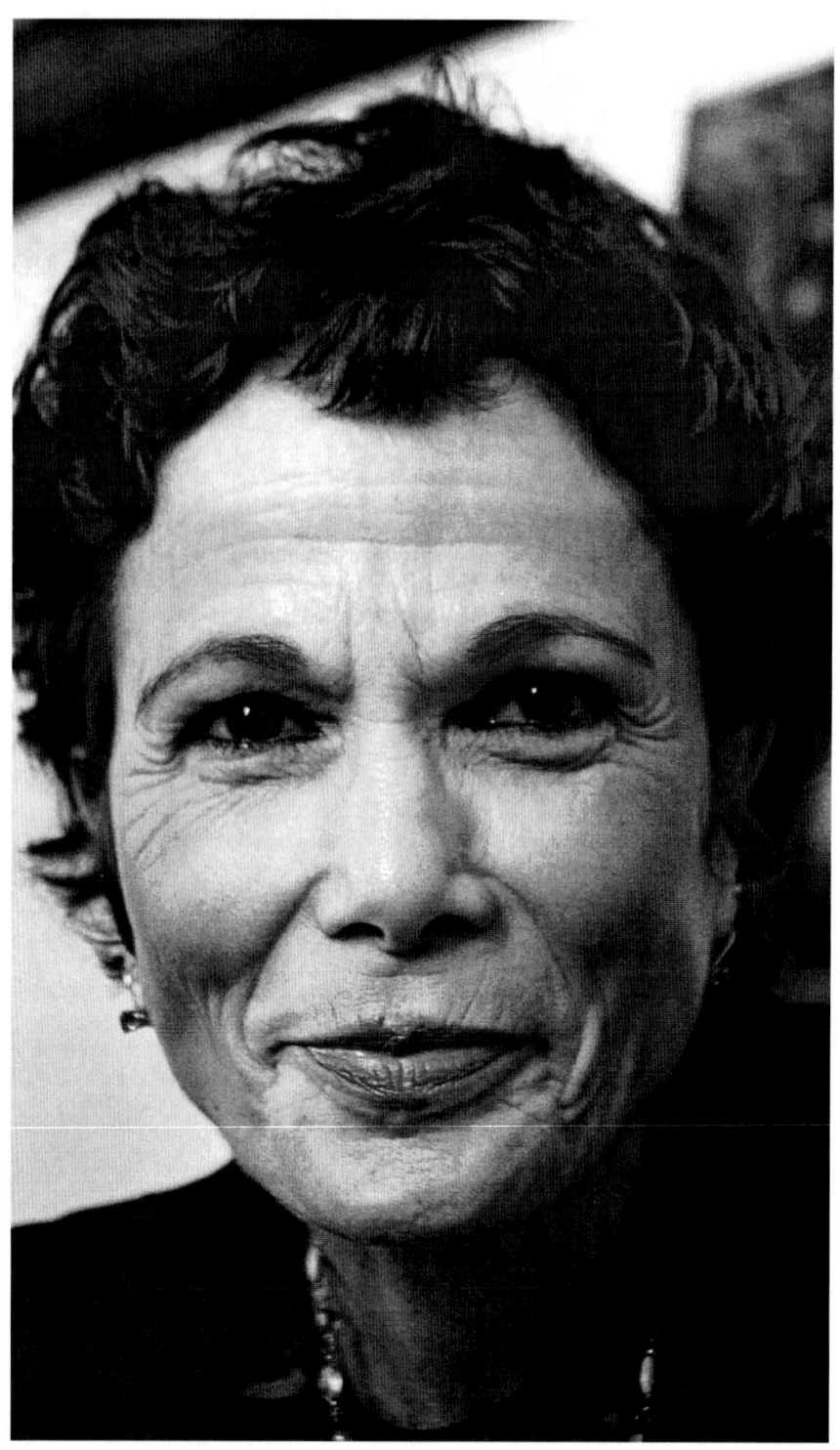

JULIA ALVAREZ

Biography

JULIA ALVAREZ was born in New York City on March 27, 1950. When she was three months old, her parents decided to move back to their native Dominican Republic, and Alvarez lived there until the age of 10. Her father had long been a part of the underground rebellion plotting to overthrow the dictatorship of Rafael Trujillo, and when the plot was discovered, her family was forced to seek asylum in the United States.

While Alvarez had taken English in school, speaking it with New Yorkers in her Catholic school classroom proved to be a challenge. She also experienced discrimination in the form of insults and taunts. To cope, she sought refuge in reading, devouring books. She knew she wanted to be a writer, but "it was the late sixties, early seventies. Afro-American writers were just beginning to gain admission into the canon. Latino literature or writers were unheard of. Writing which focused on the lives of nonwhite, nonmainstream characters was considered of ethnic interest only, the province of sociology." Nonetheless, Alvarez "kept writing, knowing that this was what was in me to do." She entered Connecticut College in 1967 and then transferred to Middlebury College, graduating in 1971. She received a master's in fine arts degree in fiction writing from Syracuse University. She then began working on a master's degree in English and American literature at Middlebury's Breadloaf School.

Throughout these early years, Alvarez supported herself by working as a writer in the schools, visiting elementary and secondary-school classrooms to teach the art of writing. She also taught high school, eventually being hired by Middlebury College to teach creative writing.

Alvarez's protagonists are usually women, often independent and struggling with their place in a society that is changing, either from within (as, for example, the Dominican Republic sheds some of its traditional gender roles) or because the protagonist finds herself in a new environment. Typically, her American-born protagonists travel to the Dominican Republic, or, alternately, they adjust to life in the United States as immigrants.

In 1991, *How the García Girls Lost Their Accents* was published to great acclaim. It won the Josephine Miles Award and was eventually named one of "Twenty-one Classics for the Twenty-first Century" by the New York Public Library. The deeply personal nature of the narrative, however, caused a rift in Alvarez's family that was slow to heal. Since the novel's publication, Alvarez began reducing her teaching commitments to write full time and has since written approximately 18 books, including poetry, cookbooks, essay collections, and works for children and young adults.

Alvarez lives with her husband, Bill Eichner, who is both an ophthalmologist and a farmer, in Vermont. Though a strict vegetarian, Alvarez helps her husband raise cows, rabbits, and chickens. They also grow almost all of their own fruits and vegetables. In 1996, Alvarez and her husband bought a coffee farm called Alta Gracía in the Dominican Republic. They are committed to cultivating and exporting organic, sustainable, shade-grown coffee and have begun a school at the site to combat widespread illiteracy.

In addition to the accolades for *How the García Girls Lost Their Accents*, Alvarez has also received myriad awards, including recognition from the American Library Association and the National Book Critics Circle.

How the García Girls Lost Their Accents
Summary and Analysis

How the García Girls Lost Their Accents has been hailed as a groundbreaking work of fiction. It relates the story of the García family, forced to flee to the United States when the father's role in a plot to overthrow the dictator is discovered. The novel consists of a series of stories that flow backward in time, from the late 1980s to the mid-1950s. The four girls—Carla, Sandra, Yolanda, and Sofía—who make up the family's younger generation deal with problems of the modern world: careers, romantic entanglements, breakdowns. Through it all, though, their Dominican heritage influences their actions and their rebellions.

The novel begins in 1989 with Yolanda, who returns to the Dominican Republic for a visit. She tells no one that she is thinking of permanently relocating there, finding her American life unsatisfying. Despite the protests of her protective extended family, she drives north in a borrowed car to assert her independence. She has a craving, an *antojo*—the title of the chapter—for guavas. She navigates the dangerous one-lane roads and stops at a roadside refreshment stand where she meets a little boy who agrees to lead her to a guava grove. They pack her trunk with the fruit, but soon after beginning the drive home, she gets a flat tire. She sends the boy for help at a nearby hacienda (whose owners are friends of her family) and remains with the car. Two men appear; initially, she is suspicious of them, taking their shyness for malice, and she pretends she does not speak Spanish. They put on the spare tire and refuse her money. She then meets the little boy halfway back to the main road; he is crying. The guard at the hacienda did not believe that there would be a woman traveling alone and beats him for lying. She drops him off, giving him much more than the dollar she promised him.

"The Kiss" is Sofía's story. Every year the four adult daughters leave their husbands to travel alone to their father's house for his birthday. This particular year, his seventieth birthday, marks a return to friendly relations between Sofía and her father after a falling out. He initially became angry because Sofía fell in love with a German named Otto. When Papi found Otto's love letters while snooping through Sofía's drawers, he learned that his daughter was no longer a virgin. After the ensuing fight, Sofía impetuously left for Germany, where she married Otto. Not even the birth of a granddaughter or Otto's position as a world-class scientist softened Papi's feelings. Her second child is a boy, however, the first born to a García in two generations, and Papi visits, swollen with pride. Sofía decides to throw him a birthday party, spending months in its planning, but Papi compliments Otto, not his daughter, for the choice of band and refuses to call Sofía by her nickname, Fifi. The party is a success, and the girls take turns kissing their blindfolded father and making him guess which one of them it was. When it is Sofía's turn, she kisses him inappropriately, licking his ear.

"The Four Girls" reveals more about the women the Garcías have become, in the form of the stories their mother tells about them. Carla is a psychologist who overanalyzes her sisters. Mami's story about Carla focuses on her insistence on having red sneakers, when all of the girls wore color-coded clothing to make Mami's housework easier. Carla insists that this stifling of their individual identities has hurt their development. Yolanda is a formerly successful poet and teacher, who is involved with a married man. Mami tells Yolanda's partner about the time that Mami and Papi lost her on a New York City bus. When they found her again, she was reciting poetry to a captive audience. Sandra has just gotten out of a mental hospital, where her parents had her committed. Her mother tells the story of Sandi's breakdown to her daughter's doctor. First, she showed signs of anorexia; then she became convinced she was turning into a monkey and wanted to read constantly to protect her brain from becoming simian too.

The chapter titled "Joe" is Yolanda's story. Obsessed with words, she became fixated on her various nicknames. In English she is "Joe." In Spanish she is Yolanda, or Yoyo, and she begins to worry that her world is as fractured as her various names and identities. Relations are strained between her and her husband, John, whose lack of imagination is apparent from the beginning of the relationship. When he starts accusing her of being irrational, and when the thought of sex with him is repulsive to her, he demands that she see a psychiatrist and creates another nickname for her—Shrinking Violet, because she seeks mental help. She finds a piece of paper on which he has listed all the pros and cons of marriage with her. After she leaves him, she has a nervous breakdown and her parents commit her to a mental hospital. While there, she falls in love with her therapist and contemplates the meaninglessness of language.

Yolanda also narrates the next chapter, "The Rudy Elmenhurst Story." This chapter is the first to be told in the first person. Yolanda describes having transferred to a coeducational college her sophomore year. She is courted by Rudy Elmenhurst, a classmate in her poetry class, who pressures her to have sex with him. But Yolanda feels she is already pushing the boundaries of what is comfortable and acceptable by drinking and enjoying the independent freedoms of college life. Ultimately, he breaks up with her, arriving at the spring dance with another girl. Yolanda gets her revenge, though, when, five years later at graduate school, he unexpectedly looks her up. When he is revealed to be as crude as ever, she kicks him out and drinks the expensive wine he leaves.

Section 2 takes place from 1960 to 1970. The girls are teenagers in "A Regular Revolution," forced to spend their summers in the Dominican Republic instead of taking advantage of their connections at boarding school to get internships. The night before they leave, they stay up late talking and gossiping. Fifi holds up a bag of marijuana and asks, should she risk taking it on their trip? Just then, they hear Mami approaching, so Fifi throws the baggie behind the dresser. The girls are in the Dominican Republic barely three weeks when Mami arrives, furious. A maid found the marijuana, and Mami demands to know whose it is. Though the girls all claim responsibility, Fifi insists it is hers. As a punishment, Mami makes her stay the year in the Dominican Republic.

At Christmas, the other three sisters are surprised to find her blending into island culture, turning into a "Spanish American Princess." But the biggest shock is that she is "seeing someone nice." The sisters are relieved to find out it is actually their illegitimate cousin Manuel, whom they nickname MG because of his initials. They find him attractive but hate the way he treats Fifi, telling her not to read, complaining that her skirt is too tight, ordering her not to flirt. Even more, they hate the way Fifi allows him to control her behavior and appearance. They discover that Manuel will not practice safe sex and even though Fifi says she has not been physically intimate with him, they see MG's car at a hotel. The sisters decide to do the only thing possible to save their sister from pregnancy and marriage. One night, they do not cover for her, returning without her and Manuel when they were supposed to have been chaperoning them, as the girls are not allowed out alone or with their boyfriends. Mami, discovering the liaison, orders her home to New York. Fifi is bereft. "Traitors," she calls her sisters.

"Daughter of Invention" takes on the story of Mami, whose name is revealed to be Laura. Far from being the docile housewife the reader has been shown up to the point in the novel, Laura is constantly creating new inventions, from a suitcase with wheels to a ticking keychain that reminds its owner to feed the meter, to instant coffee with powdered creamer already in it. When she sees a wheeled suitcase advertised and offered for sale, she loses hope. It is the Americans' country. She feels she cannot ever hope to fully infiltrate it. Though she reads the *New York Times* every night, her English is peppered with mistranslated colloquialisms and misquoted expressions. "Necessity is the daughter of invention," she misstates.

Now in the ninth grade, Yolanda is chosen to address the school on Teacher's Day but is having trouble coming up with a speech that will not make her a social pariah. She is reading Walt Whitman and, taking him as inspiration, produces an essay that advocates individuality and thinking beyond what the nuns at her Catholic school tell her. Her father is livid, claiming that the speech is disrespectful and insubordinate. He grabs it from her and tears it to pieces. Yolanda begins to cry—the speech is tomorrow—and, filled with rage, calls him the worst name she can think of: Chapita—the dictator Trujillo's nickname, the man who forced the Garcías to flee the Dominican Republic. He goes after her, but she locks herself in her room. Later, Laura comes in and together they write a less radical speech that fulfills expectations. Laura types it for Yolanda. The next day, in apology, her father brings Yolanda her own typewriter.

Carla is the eldest, and as such, when the family moves to the suburbs of Long Island to a better neighborhood, she is supposed to attend the seventh grade. But her year's class is full when they enroll her, and she is already a year older, having stayed behind a year when the family first moved to the United States. So she insists on going to a Catholic school that requires a bus ride. At first, Mami goes with her but gradually Carla walks the mile and catches the bus on her own. She does not tell her mother that each day the boys at school gang up on her at recess, calling her "spic" and pulling her socks down and her shirt up to expose her barely developed chest. She is filled with embarrassment at her own body and her own foreignness. Then one day, as she is walking home, a man motions her over to his car. Eager to be of help and thinking he needs directions, she approaches. In the car, she can see he is wearing no pants, and is masturbating. Carla is dumbstruck; she runs home and tells her mother, who calls the police. The police interview her but her English skills are poor and all Americans look alike to her. Mami then takes her to and from school every day, and the boys begin to leave her alone, but their taunting faces shouting "go back, go back," haunting her dreams and making her long to do just that.

Sandi is a picky eater, so she is not looking forward to being taken out to dinner in "Floor Show." The Garcías are in for a rare treat when they go out to a Spanish restaurant with their parents' friends the Fannings. The Fannings had visited the family in the Dominican Republic and have been instrumental in sponsoring Dr. García in the United States. Mami warns the girls to be on their best behavior, but it is clear that Mrs. Fanning is a drunk. The girls swell with pride to think that people would pay to go to a Spanish restaurant—therefore their heritage means something. When Mrs. Fanning, Papi, and Sandi go to the restroom, Sandi witnesses Mrs. Fanning kiss her father. Returning to her seat she is enthralled by the flamenco show, and, despite her mother's strict instructions, when the flamenco dancer comes to their table selling dolls, Sandi says she wants one. The embarrassed Garcías let the Fannings buy the girls four dolls. Echoing the kiss Mrs. Fanning gave her father, when prompted to thank her for her generosity, Sandi leans her doll over to kiss the woman's cheek.

The third and final section of the book takes place entirely in the Dominican Republic between the years 1956 to 1960. In this section, the privileged upbringing of the García girls contrasts greatly with their impoverished later childhood in New York. In the Dominican Republic there are maids, a family compound, and dozens of cousins next door.

"Blood of the Conquistadores" describes in detail the harassment and threats that led to the family's departure for the United States. Two members of Trujillo's secret police arrive unexpectedly. Papi hides in the crawl space created for that purpose, and Mami and the children pretend he is not home. Mami's manners prevent her from kicking the men out of the house. Instead, she sends the compound's guard to find the American consul, Victor. He became a friend of the Garcías when the State Department sent him to help organize a coup to overthrow Trujillo, which was later called off. He arrives at the house and uses his influence to send the men away. Then he announces that the visas and papers have cleared and that the Garcías are to go to New York the following morning.

At this point, the narrative shifts perspective midstory. Fifi tells of her memories of her last day on the island, which are inextricably linked with the family's maid, Chucha. Chucha arrived 30 years previously at their door, having escaped the executions of all Haitians ordered by Trujillo. She practices voodoo and sleeps in her own maid's room in a coffin, to prepare herself for death. She brings the girls a Jesus figurine while they are each packing and choosing one toy to bring to their new home. The figurine releases tears in the form of condensation, triggering the girls' own tears.

The third section of the chapter is told from Chucha's point of view. She is sad to see the family go, having served two generations. She knows, too, that she must close the house up and that she will not serve the family again. She climbs into her coffin, preparing herself for her final sleep.

"The Human Body" reveals more of the tense atmosphere under which the Garcías lived prior to their emigration. Though Yoyo's grandfather has a job at the United Nations, the family is under constant surveillance. The benefit of her grandfather's position, however, is that they get presents from his frequent trips to New York. Once, he brings back a hollow human body with removable organs that fascinates Yoyo and her closest cousin, Mundín. Another time, he brings a copy of *1,001 Arabian Nights* for Yoyo and a large mass of modeling clay for Mundín, which prompts Yoyo's jealousy. He agrees to give her some clay if she shows him "you're a girl." They go into the coal shed, which is strictly forbidden, bringing little Fifi along so she will not tell. Fifi exposes her belly button, but Yoyo, more sophisticated, pulls down her pants. Mundín gives her a dissatisfyingly small piece of clay. When they are discovered in the shed, Yolanda lies and says they were hiding from the police, which sends the family into a frenzy of worry. Mundín drops the human body model, the pieces are stepped on and mangled in the confusion, and they are never able to reassemble it.

"Still Lives" marks Sandi's turn to step forward as narrator. She has a talent for art and so her parents contract a local painter, a German native, to teach her and her cousins to paint. But the teacher is censorious, and when she punishes Sandi for drawing without permission, Sandi sneaks off to explore the grounds. She spies on the woman's husband, a sculptor, and finds him engaged in sexual activity with one of his sculptures, a nude Virgin Mary. She is so surprised that she falls off her stool, breaking her arm. She wears a cast for months, and when it comes off, her artistic ability is gone. She spots the sculptures she saw in the husband's studio at the nativity scene in the church and is startled to find her own face in the figure of the violated virgin.

Carla admits to confusion about right and wrong in her tale, "An American Surprise." Papi is back from New York with presents, and to kill time Carla talks with the new pantry maid, Gladys. This chapter emphasizes the racial and economic divide between the Garcías and their employees—Chucha and Nivea, who are Haitian, and Gladys who futilely dreams of being an American actress. The presents are disappointing—three mechanical banks that the girls soon tire of. But one bank is in the shape of the Virgin Mary. Upon the insertion of a coin, she leaps toward heaven. One night, Gladys offers her Christmas bonus to Carla in exchange for the bank. Carla decides to give it to her. When the bank is discovered missing, Mami finds it in the maid's room, and though Carla admits to giving it as a present, Gladys is fired. Afterward, the rusty bank gets stuck with Mary suspended in the middle, neither in heaven nor on earth.

The final chapter in the book, "The Drum," takes as its central image a present from the United States, a drum that Yoyo falls in love with, until a litter of kittens catches her eye. She asks advice from a passing stranger, who is inexplicably wandering around their yard. He tells her that a kitten needs its mother for at least a week. Unable to wait a week, Yoyo picks the kitten up, and to stifle its mews so its mother will not become alarmed, puts it inside her drum and begins to pound. When she reaches the laundry room, she is fearful that the mother cat will blind her, so she throws the kitten from the window and watches it limp across the garden. The cat begins to haunt her dreams, and Yoyo describes the rest of her life as a woman of nightmares and anxieties, with an irate cat wailing in the distance.

Major Themes

Julia Alvarez's novel reflects some aspects of the author's upbringing. Like the García girls, she came to the United States as a child, her family fleeing the dictatorship of Trujillo. She also left a life of privilege to struggle as an immigrant in a foreign country where she suffered discrimination. She writes in English, as she considers her Spanish not good enough, though all her books have been translated into Spanish.

Identity, Heritage, and Culture

The book's three sections correspond roughly to three major themes in the novel. The first section deals with the difficulties the García women have in finding happiness in their lives. Two spend time in mental hospitals, and while all, except Fifi, have careers, they each struggle in their personal lives. Some of this struggle can be attributed to their upbringing—their mother and father's strict rules as to how girls should act and behave created unrealistic expectations for them. Also, their mother raised them "in the American way," yet tied to Dominican customs, an education that confused them with its contradictory messages of independence and obedience, achievement and expectations. In a larger sense, the girls' struggle stands in for the pressure many immigrants' children feel to assimilate while simultaneously maintaining the cultural expectations of their parents' homeland.

Another reason for their troubles, Alvarez suggests, is the changing roles of women in today's society. Yolanda, especially, has a difficult time reconciling her intelligence and her career with her husband's expectations. Sandi bows to modern expectations of beauty, developing anorexia. Because the book takes on so many themes, this theme is hinted at but not fully explored. The girls' mother, because of her role as a housewife, is similarly dismissed. Mami does not want to return to the Dominican Republic, because, even though they had much more domestic help there, she felt stifled by her life of privilege and the more rigidly defined gender roles.

An additional theme in the first section of the book is how grown-up children deal with their older parents. The García girls treat their father with deference but are frustrated by his rigid nature and his old-fashioned ways. The girls are embarrassed by Mami's talkativeness and her constant storytelling, but it is through her highly verbal presence that they are able to piece together their childhood.

Coming of Age

The second section of the book takes as its major themes the girls' coming of age, their assimilation into American society, and their budding sexuality. The girls experience discrimination, from the lady downstairs who calls them "spics" to the taunting of classmates. There is the added embarrassment of not speaking English, of being held back a grade because of language difficulties, and of having overly strict parents. The girls try to negotiate their freedom to be typical American teenagers, full of rebellion and self-discovery, even as they try to make their parents happy.

Sexuality is omnipresent in this section. Carla is teased because of her developing body and her hairy legs. Sandi witnesses her father's minor infidelity. Sexuality is also revealed to have its violent and exploitative sides as well. Carla crosses paths with a sexual predator, while Yolanda's boyfriend dumps her because she will not have sex with him. Implicit in these experiences is the stereotype that Hispanic women are "hot-blooded, being Spanish and all, and that under all the Catholic [morality], you'd be really free." This skewed viewpoint contrasts with the message of strict chastity professed by the Catholic Church.

The Dominican Experience

The third section addresses larger themes of the Dominican experience. First, the social position and wealth of the García family (and their de la Torre cousins) contrasts with the poverty of the new immigrants. The Garcías in the Dominican Republic have a vast estate that abuts the dictator's property. They enjoy chauffeurs, several maids, parties, imported chocolates, and frequent trips to the United States. The girls have no problem ordering around the maids and servants, taking their privileged lives for granted.

Another undercurrent in this section of Alvarez's novel is the racism that is accepted in Dominican society. Haitians, who share the island with the Dominican Republic, are discriminated against because of their African heritage. Nivea's mother rubs cream into her skin to turn it whiter, and Sandi is praised as the most beautiful, because it is she who has inherited the blond hair and light skin of her distant Swedish ancestor. It is not until they reach the United States and are discriminated against because of their Hispanic heritage, that they become aware of being victims, as well as perpetrators of racism.

Perhaps the most significant tension in the novel's third section is the constant threat of exposure to Trujillo's regime. Even in the stories that do not address politics specifically, the eerie presence of the SIM, Trujillo's secret police, looms. Fifi almost gets her father killed by being rude to a policeman. Yolanda is repentant for having set off a firecracker near Trujillo's grandson and for having bragged about their father's firearm, for which she received a beating. Just mentioning the *guardia* (police) gets Yoyo out of trouble by turning the family's focus away from her misdeed. This constant fear is harmful and debilitating, as are Papi's worries years later about his relatives who have been arrested, interrogated, or killed.

Because this book is so rich with themes, despite its short length, it is considered a masterwork of Hispanic literature. Alvarez has succeeded, with her first major literary effort, to create a sympathetic portrait of the Dominican experience in the United States.

In the Time of the Butterflies
Summary and Analysis

In the Time of the Butterflies recounts the true story of the Mirabal sisters, who were killed in their struggle against Trujillo's dictatorial regime in the Dominican Republic. Alvarez imagines the four women's motivations and struggles as she provides a fictionalized account of the "Butterflies," the regime's opposition leaders. The book is divided into four parts; each is narrated by each of the four sisters in turn. The novel opens in 1994 as the only surviving sister, Dedé, is tending her garden, waiting for a *"gringa dominicana"* interviewer, whose questions trigger Dedé's reminiscences. She thinks of the time her father told the sisters' fortunes. Only Dedé's was specific: "She'll bury us all in silk and pearls." Dedé muses that the prophecy has come true.

In 1938, Dedé is an adolescent sent with her sisters to a Catholic boarding school. It is there that she begins to suspect, through a friend's experiences, that the Trujillo regime is not the benevolent presidency she had thought. Rafael Leonidas Trujillo took power in 1930 in a military coup and subsequently ruled the country with a tenacious grip. It was mandatory to have his portrait hanging in each house, and any resistance, even slander or an offhand comment, was a punishable offense. Trujillo's power and cruelty begin to more profoundly impact Dedé when a classmate becomes the leader's mistress, and the girl disappears into obscurity. At a play they are performing for Trujillo and his son, Dedé's classmate threatens the dictator with a bow and arrow. The conflict is diffused, but afterward Dedé feels as though she is "looking at the world through a curtain of tears."

María Teresa, known as Mate, narrates chapter 3 in the form of diary entries recorded during the years 1945-46. In contrast to her more serious sisters, the youngest is preoccupied with frivolous adolescent concerns: clothes and boys. Through her, the reader learns that her older sister Minerva is increasingly politically active, while the eldest, Patría, has married. The diary ends when Minerva insists on burying it after Mate includes mention of Minerva's resistance activities.

Chapter 4 is told by the deeply religious Patría. The pride of the nuns at the school, Patría contemplates joining the sisterhood, until she falls in love with Pedrito and realizes that her calling is to motherhood. When her son is stillborn, though, her faith is tested. Though she agrees with Minerva that the Trujillo regime is corrupt, she justifies it: "El Jefe was no saint, everyone knew that, but among the *bandidos* that had been in the National Palace, this one at least was building churches and schools, paying off our debts." She continues to reason with Minerva, "We women shouldn't get involved." But of course, Minerva does just that, taking on the code name *mariposa* or butterfly. The sisters meet Virgilio (Lío) Morales, a leader of the resistance movement. He and Minerva form an attachment that is both political and romantic and begin subversive activities designed to topple the regime. Dedé is jealous of Minerva's relationship, even though a man named Jaimito asks her to marry him. When Lío becomes wanted by the government, he entrusts Dedé with a letter asking Minerva to seek asylum with him. Motivated by envy and love, Dedé burns the letter.

Minerva grows increasingly dissatisfied with her life. Forbidden by her father to attend the university, she spots his car at a peasant's house and recognizes "Mirabal eyes" in the four young girls outside the house. She realizes that her father has been having an affair. She searches in his armoire and discovers letters that Lío has written her that her father has confiscated. In addition to anger, she feels pity for her father, who has made so many "shabby choices." She is meanwhile invited to a party thrown by Trujillo. It would be against the law to decline, and so the entire family attends the event.

At the dance, Minerva tells Trujillo of her dream to go to law school. When he replies with a vulgar comment, she slaps him before she can stop herself. The family uses the cover of a sudden thundershower to escape, but they are paralyzed with fear. Insulting the leader can invite any sort of punishment, including death. They immediately pen an apology, but the police come anyway, taking Minerva's father to jail. As he is taken away, he asks Minerva to look after his other family.

In jail, the father suffers a heart attack, and though he is released, he dies soon after. Mate picks up the narrative again in the form of a new diary. She relates that Minerva has attended university and married a classmate, Manolo, though Trujillo declines to grant her a license to practice law. True to Mate's nature, her diary is filled with news of boyfriends, clothes, and gifts, though she also relates Minerva and Manolo's rebellious activities. When a young man comes to the house to make a secret arms delivery, Mate falls in love and begins to aid in the struggle, working to coordinate arms deliveries and construct bombs. A second mariposa, thus, joins the resistance.

Patría's commitment to her faith and to staying out of politics is tested when her son begins to speak of the revolution. Fidel Castro's takeover of Cuba gives everyone in the resistance new hope. Patría at first offers her land to Minerva as a place to hold secret meetings, then becomes increasingly involved, even as she is pregnant with a late-in-life baby whom she will name after Che Guevara and Fidel's brother, Raúl. After witnessing the government massacre members of the resistance not much older than her son, she decides to take action, using her land as a meeting place and an arms depot. When her husband finds out, he is furious.

Dedé's husband says he will leave her if she joins the resistance, and she uses his ultimatum as an excuse not to join her sisters. Unhappy in her marriage, she decides to leave, but she is prevented when the secret police arrest her sisters' husbands, followed by Minerva and Mate. Only she and Patria are left to petition for their release. Dedé and her husband draw closer together.

The illegitimate Mirabal sister brings news of the imprisoned women, who are sent food and clothing. Meanwhile, Patría flirts with the local policeman, securing her son's release and a pass to see her sisters. She asks God to take her instead of her son. Mate's diary tells of her harsh treatment in prison. Starved, denied medical treatment and clothing, she hints at even harsher treatment—a gang rape witnessed by her husband. She is able to sneak out a report of their treatment to a visiting international civil rights organization, and soon afterward, both sisters are released into house arrest. Minerva's reintegration is not smooth. Weakened by her captivity, she wilts under house arrest. She is only allowed to go to church, where she is constantly reminded of her ordeal by people calling her by her revolutionary name Mariposa. The sisters are allowed to visit their captured husbands, who are despondent, convinced they are going to die in prison. The revolutionary cells have mostly been eradicated; the sisters are too prominent to agitate any more dissent, and any hope of being helped by the United States falls away after American relations with Cuba disintegrate.

When the men are transferred to a distant prison, the sisters hire a driver to take them over the dangerous mountain pass to visit their husbands. Stopping one day to shop for purses, the women are slipped a message of warning by a clerk. Suddenly, the seemingly harmless hitchhiking soldier they picked up appears to be a government operative. The signs are ominous, but they are able to visit the men and start back over the pass for home, though it is late and dark.

Later, Dedé is able to piece together the story of the rest of their journey. The sisters were stopped on the road and strangled, their driver as well. The police put the bodies into the car and drove it to a precipice, pushing it over to make it look like an accident. Dedé realizes her father's prophecy has come true: Dedé has buried them all. Though she wants to join her sisters in death, Jaimito says that "this is your martyrdom, Dedé, to be alive without them."

Dedé survives as the living "oracle" to the memory of the Mariposas. Minerva's husband is killed in a suicide mission, and Patría's husband remarries. Dedé's husband moves to New York, sending back money to keep the farm operating. Though Dedé lives to see her children, nieces, and nephews grow up and witnesses the Trujillo regime fall after 31 years and the subsequent free elections, she questions the nature of her sisters' sacrifices: "[W]as it for this, the sacrifice of the butterflies?"

Major Themes

The Historical Past

Alvarez fictionalizes four major figures in Dominican history. When asked why she chose to tell this story, she said, "needless to say, this was a story I felt compelled to write.... My father was part of the same group as the Mirabal sisters and we got out and they didn't get out. There's always the responsibility of the survivors to tell the story of those who didn't make it." Alvarez, thus, feels the need to give voice to the lives and legend of the Mirabal sisters.

Alvarez creates rounded and distinct characters in her imagined versions of the Mirabal sisters. Each has a different approach to living under Trujillo. Minerva is the rebel, arguing with her father and her sisters. Her revolutionary activities begin in high school, and her struggle to educate herself and her illegitimate sisters can be seen as representing the challenges facing the modern woman. She feels the call to sacrifice acutely, asking Patría to keep her son while she plots a revolution. Therefore, she puts aside traditional female values of motherhood to fight for a greater cause. She is also willing to sacrifice anything for her education and her political beliefs.

Patría, meanwhile, is devoted to her religion. She believes the best in everyone and is reluctant to believe that Trujillo's regime is anything but benevolent. When the evidence to the contrary becomes overwhelming, she still does not feel the call to action until her son is taken and she begins to identify with the Virgin Mary. Though her faith is shaken throughout her ordeal, it is during a religious retreat, when she witnesses rebels being killed, that she reconciles her faith with the revolutionary cause.

María Teresa is the frivolous daughter, caught up in hair ribbons and boys. In prison, she says "after you lose your fear, the hardest thing here is the lack of beauty." She enters the revolution because of a romantic crush on a young man who later becomes her husband. She is the most stereotypically "feminine" of the sisters, giggling and concerned about her appearance.

Dedé, the main narrator, is perhaps the most flawed of the sisters. She uses her husband's threat as an excuse to hide her fear and her reluctance to join her sisters in rebellion. Yet she, too, is dragged into the battle. Even inaction can be action. She becomes the main narrator, as she is the one left alive to tell the tale. She is also perhaps the most trustworthy narrator, as she is not motivated by political ideology to tell her story. To the end, she does not want to be a hero. She agrees to an interview but seems embarrassed by the attention.

Alvarez says the creation of a character based on historical fact is the same as creating a character from imagination. "To saturate oneself in the creating of the character and putting them on paper. That's true of totally fictional or historical characters. You've got some of the facts, testimonies, points of view, and then you absorb all of this to turn it into something. [T]he challenge is to make that voice come alive on paper. With a historical character, it's just different kind of information that you have to give voice to." Therefore, she approaches the Mirabal sisters with the same authorial stance as her fictional characters.

The Role of Women in Dominican Society

Women are central to the narrative. Though men play an important role in the revolution, Alvarez's portrait is unique in that, in a male-dominated society, the main rebels are sisters. Acting from their positions of relative powerlessness, they are able to effect more change than their male counterparts. They ignore their husbands' overprotectiveness, consider leaving them (itself a radical act), and actively lie to their husbands when their convictions necessitate it. In some ways, this novel is about the various forms of female power.

In that regard, however, the work can also be seen as a cautionary tale. Three of the sisters die, suggesting that this is the fate of women who actively resist. Alvarez is commenting on the lack of options for women and not only in the period in which she writes about. By bringing the narrative into the present day with Dedé and her niece, Alvarez ties the story to women's contemporary struggle for equality and fulfillment. She is proud that "the United Nations has even declared November 25th the International Day Against Violence Against Women because of the Mirabal sisters." Alvarez considers the story of these women not only necessary to relate but important for the understanding of the Dominican experience. Though the American immigrant experience is not reflected in the novel, as in many of the other works discussed in this volume, Alvarez's imagining of the historical events offers the background against which Dominicans were struggling, the reality that thousands of Dominican immigrants left behind.

OSCAR HIJUELOS

Biography

CONSIDERED, ALONG WITH Rudolfo Anaya, one of the godfathers of Hispanic-American literature, Oscar Hijuelos was born August 24, 1951, in New York City. When he was four years old, his father, a cook at the Biltmore Hotel, sent him, his brother, and their mother to Cuba to see relatives. During the trip, Hijuelos developed a kidney infection and then spent months in a hospital when he returned to the United States, an experience he writes about in his first novel. He was forced to speak English in the hospital and credits the time there with perfecting his English.

Hijuelos grew up in West Harlem in New York City and attended public schools. His father instilled in him a strong work ethic, while his mother's poetic turns of phrase made the Cuban landscape and dialect a rich source of inspiration. He graduated from the City University of New York in 1975. He received an M.A. in creative writing a year later. At school, he was mentored by Donald Barthleme, who noted his talent and encouraged his career. While he gained relative success when he was still young, Hijuelos worked for years in an advertising firm, writing fiction at night. He also held a series of the odd jobs that many writers pursue until they are established. He worked in inventory control, sold curtain rods at Macy's department store, and was a farmhand in Wisconsin.

His first novel, *Our House in the Last World*, was published in 1983. That book, which included an episode paralleling the author's childhood hospitalization, depicts the lives of the members of a Cuban-American family in New York's Spanish Harlem neighborhood in the 1940s. The alcoholic father's influence on his family and their resulting poverty form the background for an examination of assimilation and discrimination in the United States. The book received excellent reviews, and in 1985 Hijuelos won a National Endowment for the Arts fellowship followed by a Rome Prize and a Guggenheim Fellowship. Each allowed him to devote more time to writing and to researching mambo music and the club scene of the 1950s for his next book, *The Mambo Kings Play Songs of Love*. When the book was released, few predicted the impact it would have. "I remember being told, when the novel came out, 'Minority novels don't sell. Period,'" Hijuelos said. "That's what you hear if you're Hispanic. 'Punto.' Forget it, baby."

Despite the anticipated obstacles, the book won the Pulitzer Prize in 1990 (he was the first Hispanic American to win the award), was a best-seller, and was translated into more than 20 languages. When a film version came out in 1994, the public rediscovered the book. The success of *Mambo Kings* catapulted Hijuelos into the literary stratosphere. He has since been compared to other prominent Latin American writers, though his style is more of a lyrical realism than the magical realism, with its elements of fantasy, that characterizes the works of others. Music features as a prominent motif in his works. Hijuelos also fictionalizes real people, including Desi Arnez (though he changes his name to Arnaz), the husband of Lucille Ball and one of the stars of television show *I Love Lucy*, who is a secondary character in the book. Because the novel's mambo scenes are so realistic, the bandleader Gloria Parker sued him for defamation. The case was eventually dismissed, but it increased publicity for the book.

Hijuelos went on to write several more books, including *The Fourteen Sisters of Emilio Montez O'Brien* (1993), *Mr. Ives' Christmas* (1995), *Empress of the Splendid Season* (1999), and *A Simple Habana Melody: From When the World Was Good* (2002). His first young adult book, *Dark Dude*, was published in 2008. Hijuelos occasionally teaches as a visiting writer at various universities. He is married to Lori Marie Carlson, a writer, editor, and translator, and they live in New York.

The Mambo Kings Play Songs of Love
Summary and Analysis

The novel begins with narrator Eugenio Castillo remembering an afternoon when he was a child. The landlady calls; Eugenio's uncle and father are on television again: a rerun of the one episode of *I Love Lucy* on which Cesar and Nestor appeared, singing their bolero hit, "Beautiful Maria of My Soul." Cesar, who in his present state is decrepit and perpetually hung over, is almost unrecognizable as the healthy young man on the television.

Like a record, *The Mambo Kings* is divided into two sides. At the beginning of Side A, Cesar checks in to the Hotel Splendour. He plans to lose himself in his memories with the help of records and whiskey. It is clear that he is near the end of his life, an alcoholic revisiting the past as he drinks his last few dregs. Accordingly, his memories travel back and forth in time. His recollections begin appropriately with his childhood, he and his brother Nestor growing up on a farm in Cuba. They eventually formed a small mambo group and moved to New York in 1949.

The pair named their band the Mambo Kings but were forced to work in a meatpacking plant during the day before finding success. Before coming to the United States, Cesar was in Julián García's orchestra. He married the niece of the orchestra leader but was unfaithful to her. When she discovered his infidelity, she left him, bearing his daughter Mariela shortly afterward. Cesar has sent her presents and visited over the years, but the distance that exists between them is one of his biggest regrets.

Cesar's nickname, the Mambo King, is derived from his sexual prowess and voraciousness. Many of his memories are of the women he has been with. He even believes he once stayed with one woman, Vanna Vane, in the very room he has checked into to die. The fact that he is now increasingly impotent is the final indication to him that his life is over.

He also reminisces about his brother Nestor. Once, Nestor was walking down the street, when he prevented a woman from being beaten by her boyfriend. Nestor started a relationship with her, the María of their successful song. Turning to Cesar for advice, Nestor is advised to show her who the man of the relationship is, in other words, hit her. María leaves him. When he finds her, she has married the boyfriend he was protecting her from when they met. Nestor is inconsolable. For the rest of his life he remains in love with her, carrying her picture around and rewriting her ballad 44 times.

Nestor's perspective is the subject of the next section of the book. In 1950, Nestor is so taken with a woman he sees on the bus that he follows her. Her name is Delores, an intelligent woman who cleans house for a rich man in Manhattan. Nestor invites her to hear him play at the Imperial Ballroom. Delores has lived a sheltered life, moving to the United States with her father and serving as his homemaker. Eventually, her fun-loving sister Ana Maria joined her in New York. Ana Maria would go out dancing, while Delores stayed home to read. But on this particular weekend, Delores asks if Ana Maria will accompany her to see the musician she has met.

When Delores discovers she is pregnant, Nestor marries her out of duty, but he is still in love with María. Delores gives birth to a son, Eugenio, the narrator of the book. Three years later, they have a daughter, Leticia.

Cesar then recalls the year when it seemed the band had finally found success. In 1955, the Mambo Kings are traveling the country after establishing a name for themselves in the New York dance halls. They have even found an audience with their recordings, but Nestor's anxiety and depression do not allow him to enjoy the success.

One night at a popular New York mambo club, Desi Arnaz and Lucille Ball arrive to hear the famous Mambo Kings. Afterward, the four share a drink, and it is revealed that Desi is from the same small Cuban town as the Castillo brothers and had played with Julián García's band as well. Desi asks if they will appear on *I Love Lucy* to play "Beautiful Maria of My Soul." Drunk and happy, the brothers invite the television stars back to their house in the Bronx for a late-night Cuban dinner. Delores is shocked but thrilled to have two such important people in her house and immediately begins to fry pork chops.

The brothers travel to Los Angeles and are wined and dined in preparation for their appearance on the show. Cesar enjoys himself, but Nestor is plagued by anxiety. They perform well, and Cesar tries to sleep with as many women as he can, while Nestor remains faithful to his loveless marriage.

Suddenly, the brothers are famous. They are also financially successful, with a national tour and the royalties on re-recordings of "Beautiful Maria of My Soul." Cesar purchases a fancy new car, with the intention of using it to seduce more women. One cold night, he is kissing his girlfriend Vanna while Nestor drives them home after a performance. Nestor hits a patch of ice and crashes into a tree, dying instantly. Vanna and Cesar are unharmed. Cesar is distraught over his brother's death. He waits several hours before going home to tell his sister-in-law and niece and nephew about Nestor's death. On the day of the funeral, Nestor meets Vanna for sex, which he uses, as usual, to dull his pain.

Cesar returns to his music and playing the bongos but fears he has lost his passion for it. He feels so guilty about Nestor's death that he wishes he could trade places with him. Every time the replacement trumpet player flubs the solo in "Beautiful Maria of My Soul," the wound reopens. Finally, the other band members suggest a vacation. When he makes a drunken pass at Delores, he knows it is time to get away.

Cesar returns to Cuba where his brothers, mother, and the household help welcome him. He sees his ex-wife, happily remarried and pregnant, and his teenage daughter, who is a gifted ballerina. The only one who is not overjoyed is Cesar's father, who has always been cruel. Cesar recalls one time his father chased him through the sugarcane with a machete. When the father's foot became impaled on a stick, he begged Cesar to help him, but Cesar thought it was a trick. Finally, realizing it was not a ruse, he carried his father home, but as soon as the wound was bandaged, his father came after Cesar again.

Cesar joins the merchant marines and spends several years sailing around the world. When he returns, he moves back in with Delores, who is now remarried, and Nestor's children. Delores, however, has changed; she no longer allows him to use the apartment as a crash pad for drunken musicians. She wants him to move out, but his inertia keeps him on her sofa for several months, when he is not spending the night with a woman.

Finally, Cesar sees a "Help Wanted" sign in his building. The landlady has always had a crush on Cesar and tells him she needs a maintenance man. Cesar tries it out and finds that he likes it. A fringe benefit of the job is an apartment of his own, so he can be close to his family without living with them. He spends a lot of time in his basement office. Soon, people ask him when he will revive the Mambo Kings.

Side B of the novel finds Cesar back in the hotel. He has another drink, despite his doctor saying that Cesar's organs are starting to fail and that he should quit immediately. He has recently been released from the hospital, where even in his weakened state he hit on the nurses.

Cesar begins to play again, while keeping his job as a superintendent. His friend offers to buy a nightclub and let Cesar run it. Cesar hires Eugenio to help him, but Eugenio's generosity eventually threatens the business. He houses and gives money to recently arrived Cuban musicians and gives away more alcohol than he charges for. The club is failing, so the owner assumes control and turns it into a rock and roll venue. The transition breaks Cesar's heart, as does the news that his friend is selling drugs out of the club. Meanwhile, in Cuba, the political situation is oppressive. Cesar's brothers write him to ask for money. Cesar tries to get Mariela out of Cuba, but she is happily ensconced as the director of a ballet company and the stepdaughter of a high-ranking official in Fidel Castro's government.

Cesar returns to the present. He said his goodbyes before checking into the hotel, giving away his recordings. He worries about Eugenio, in whom he recognizes Nestor's depression, and asks Eugenio not to forget him. Cesar's mind then becomes a jumble of randomly recalled memories. He thinks of the time he was romantically involved with his friend's wife and concedes that much of his life has been in pursuit of or ruined by sex. There was a forty-year-old virgin, Celia, whom Cesar raped and who wanted to marry him, and a cast of others whose names and faces he can no longer recall. His former behavior, nonetheless, fills him with regret.

The third section is called "Near the End, While Listening to the Wistful 'Beautiful Maria of My Soul.'" It is late in the evening, and Cesar recalls the final chapter of his life. After 20 years as a maintenance man, he finds a degree of contentment, but he is lonely without a family of his own. Then he meets Lydia, a woman half his age with whom he strikes up a relationship. He happily spends most evenings at her house with her children. Cesar is obsessed, though, by the idea that Lydia will leave him for a younger man. Though he is still virile, his body is slowly starting to fail him.

As Cesar grows increasingly ill, he begins to hallucinate. He thinks he sees Desi Arnaz and even Nestor, who has been dead nearly 30 years. Cesar has nightmares in which women tell him he is going to die. He begins to take painkillers for his stomach ailment, which he mixes with alcohol. One night, Lydia stands him up in order to take her son to the emergency room, and Cesar, jealous, ends the relationship. He realizes that his anger is due in part to his abuse of substances, but Lydia is nonetheless disgusted by the decrepit, addictive man.

From his hotel bed, Cesar becomes delirious, awash in memories. He is found dead the next morning, the handwritten lyrics to "Beautiful Maria of My Soul" on the nightstand.

Eugenio narrates the last section, a brief epilogue. At Cesar's funeral, Desi Arnaz sends flowers and an invitation to Cesar's surviving relatives, so Eugenio goes to Desi's house. The star invites him in and shows him his Cuban-style house. Eugenio gives Desi recordings of "Beautiful Maria of My Soul." He stays for lunch, happy that Desi's attachment to the Castillo brothers is genuine.

After the meal, the talk turns more serious. Desi tells Eugenio that he used to believe he would be immortal. Eugenio has a fantasy that Desi embraces him and tells Eugenio he loves him, acting as a standin for the father that Eugenio lost when he was so young. Desi goes to take a phone call, and Eugenio imagines his father and Cesar, young, having coffee with Lucille Ball and a young Desi Arnaz. He imagines all of them in the scene from the Castillo brothers' one *I Love Lucy* appearance. The brothers are performing with the orchestra at the Tropicana (the club owned by Desi's character, Ricky Ricardo) and Cesar's and Nestor's hearts are so large that they escape their bodies and float away together.

Major Themes

Love and Intimacy

Love plays a major role in *The Mambo Kings Play Songs of Love*; the word even appears in the title. Love is idealized in the book and often goes unrealized or unappreciated. Nestor is the most extreme example. He remains devoted to a woman who spurned him his entire life. He rewrites the song he wrote about her 44 times to try to approach the perfection he saw in her.

On the flip side is Cesar, whose appetite for having sex with multiple partners is insatiable. Yet, he envies Nestor his family, to the point that he desires Delores, even though he is not physically attracted to her. Cesar is obsessed with sex, yet it does not provide him the intimacy or emotional comfort he craves.

Sexuality is another major theme in the book. Cesar spends much of his last evening recalling the shapes and situations of the many, many women he had been with. Much of the book is dedicated to graphic descriptions of his sexual prowess, but his pursuit of physical pleasure for its own sake ends only in sadness and loneliness. His attitude toward life and women fails all the characters in the book. The one time Nestor tries to emulate and apply his brother's particular code of machismo, he succeeds in driving away the only woman he has ever loved. Cesar, too, loses his love because he is proud and insecure.

Despite a yearning for connection and intimacy, both brothers suffer from bouts of depression, which can be viewed as Hijuelos's comment on masculine vulnerability and frailty, despite a societal pressure to be strong and emotionally resilient. Nestor contemplates suicide several times and becomes the sole victim of the car accident. Cesar's complete disregard for and indifference to his health ends his life prematurely. Much of the depression and ill health in the novel stems from the disappointment the brothers feel at their lack of success and thwarted hopes.

Music and Language

What makes the novel stand out is its style. Like mambo music, the prose is fast paced and rhythmic. It lurches forward then loops back, mimicking the structure of a song or an improvised musical solo. Just as the novel has an A side and a B side, like one of the Mambo Kings' recordings, so, too, does the prose follow the same metaphoric pattern. Thus, Hijuelos has managed to create a tribute to the very style of music his narrative celebrates, able to replicate and reproduce on the page, through the use of words, the qualities of music or the experience of witnessing a performance by a lively, talented mambo band.

SANDRA CISNEROS

Biography

SANDRA CISNEROS considers herself a Latina, a Chicana, and a feminist. Born on December 20, 1954, in Chicago, Illinois, Cisneros had a disrupted childhood. Her father was a Mexican native from a wealthy family, who loved to travel and worked as an upholsterer. Her mother was an American of Mexican ancestry who worked in a factory. Cisneros was the only girl among seven children, and the family moved frequently from neighborhood to neighborhood and from Chicago to Mexico. Money was always tight.

In 1969, her parents borrowed money to purchase a bungalow in a Puerto Rican neighborhood in Chicago's North Side. There, Cisneros was finally able to put down roots. She describes the house as unattractive and similar to the one she imagines in *The House on Mango Street*.

Cisneros credits her mother with instilling in her a love of literature. Cisneros's mother made sure that her young daughter had a library card and did not interrupt her if Sandra was reading. Additionally, her mother freed her from the gender stereotypes that, with six brothers around, might have consigned her to traditional roles. These brothers also helped Cisneros develop her writing skills. "You had to be fast and you had to be funny—you had to be a *storyteller*," she has said. Some of her early influences were Lewis Carroll and Donald Justice, as well as the leaders of the Chicano poetry movement in Chicago.

Cisneros attended Loyola University, graduating in 1976. While there, she was encouraged to write, and she subsequently enrolled in the prestigious University of Iowa Writers' Workshop, graduating with a master of fine arts degree in 1978. The Iowa years were hard on Cisneros. Most of her classmates were white, came from privileged backgrounds, and were not writing the kinds of stories she was interested in. She became friends with Joy Harjo, a Native American poet, who also wrote from a perspective outside the canon. It was in Iowa, though, that Cisneros first hit upon the idea of using a home as a central metaphor for her first book, *The House on Mango Street*, published in 1984.

The House on Mango Street was a critical success, winning the American Book Award from the Before Columbus Foundation. Cisneros was subsequently awarded a series of grants, including a National Endowment for the Arts grant, a Lannan Foundation grant, and a MacArthur Fellowship. She has also been a visiting professor at numerous universities.

Following the success of *The House on Mango Street*, Cisneros continued to explore other genres, writing volumes of poetry and additional works of fiction. *My Wicked Wicked Ways*, a collection of poetry, was published in 1987, followed by *Woman Hollering Creek*, an acclaimed collection of short fiction, which came out in 1991. Of her work, she says, "I wanted to write stories that were a cross between poetry and fiction. . . . Except I wanted to write a collection which could be read at any random point without having any knowledge of what came before or after. Or that could be read in a series to tell one big story. I wanted stories like poems, compact and lyrical and ending with a reverberation." Other works include *Loose Woman: Poems* (1994), *Hairs: Pelitos* (1994), and *Caramelo* (a novel, 2002).

Cisneros has continued to be a voice for Chicano literature in the United States, claiming that Hispanics "are still the illegal aliens of the literary world." She has also continued to forge an identity for herself in her personal life free from the constraints of society's expectations. She is "nobody's wife [and] nobody's mother" and lives in Texas on the banks of the San Antonio River, where she devotes her time to writing and is active in Mujeres de la paz, an organization that fights for the rights of women, especially those who have been victimized by war.

The House on Mango Street
Summary and Analysis

In *The House on Mango Street*, Sandra Cisneros creates a novel in short vignettes. Esperanza (which in English "means hope. In Spanish it means too many letters") and her family move to a house on Mango Street in Chicago after years of moving from apartment to apartment. Though the family has dreamed for years of living in a real home, the house on Mango Street is a ramshackle disappointment in a bad neighborhood.

Each of the 42 chapters is a short story. Some relate stories of Esperanza's childhood and that of her younger sister Magdalena ("Nenny") and her friends, two sisters named Rachel and Lucy. Esperanza feels simultaneously burdened by Nenny and also glad to have a partner, defending her little sister against the neighborhood taunts.

Other chapters in the novel relate stories about various residents of the neighborhood. There is Alicia, who has enrolled in college and is a subject of envy as well as derision. She is also deathly afraid of mice. There is sophisticated Marin, a lonely teenager living with her aunt and uncle, forced to babysit around the clock and eventually sent back to Puerto Rico as punishment for her short skirts and beautiful eyes. Meme Ortiz is a neglected child, who breaks both arms in a Tarzan jumping contest.

As the book progresses, Esperanza grows up and grows increasingly interested in boys. She is fascinated by Sally, a physically abused girl, who dresses in black and lets the boys kiss her. Against this backdrop, Esperanza becomes a young adult. She notices that her body is changing; she develops hips. "One day you wake up and they are there." Men and boys start to notice her and make unwanted advances. In "Red Clowns," Esperanza is sexually assaulted while she waits for Sally at an amusement park. She tries to blame the rape on Sally: "You never came for me. Sally Sally a hundred times. Why didn't you hear me when I called? Why didn't you tell them to leave me alone?" Esperanza is haunted by her attacker's words: "He said I love you, I love you Spanish girl."

Included in the vignettes is an indictment of how women are treated in traditional Mexican culture. Men are mostly portrayed as abusive or abandoning. Minerva, a neighbor, kicks her husband out of the house, only to take him back after he beats her. Rafaela is locked in her house because her husband is afraid she will leave him; Esperanza delivers her coconut and papaya juice by sending it up a rope ladder. Balancing this criticism of abusive, insensitive men is Esperanza's observation that the women keep taking back their abusive partners. When Sally runs to Esperanza's house to escape her father's blows, he follows her, apologizing. Sally calls him "Daddy," which surprises Esperanza.

As the novel progresses, Esperanza feels increasingly desperate to escape the world of Mango Street. She is embarrassed when a nun is astonished that she lives in such a bad neighborhood, and she tries to get permission to eat lunch at school so she does not to have to return home midday. But "like it or not," says Alicia, a neighbor, "you are Mango Street and you'll come back too." Three fortune-telling sisters reiterate the point. "When you leave you must remember to come back for the others." But Esperanza has larger plans. "I like to tell stories." These stories, and her intelligence, will be her means of escape. She dreams of her own house. "Not a flat. Not an apartment in back. Not a man's house. Not a daddy's. A house all my own."

The book ends with the chapter "Mango Says Goodbye Sometimes." In it, Esperanza says she "makes a story for my life." She "will pack my bags of books and paper. One day I will say goodbye to Mango." Still, she predicts that she will come back "for the ones I left behind. For the ones that cannot out."

Major Themes

Strength and Resolve

One recurring theme throughout the novel that develops along with the protagonist is Esperanza's strength and resolve. In the chapter "Four Skinny Trees," Esperanza compares herself to the trees growing on her block. "They are the only ones who understand me. I am the only one who understands them." She draws her inspiration from them. "Their strength is secret. They send ferocious roots beneath the ground. They grow up and they grow down and grab the earth between their hairy toes and bite the sky with violent teeth and never quit their anger. This is how they keep."

Esperanza explains how the trees mimic her determination to overcome her surroundings. "When I am too sad and too skinny to keep keeping, when I am a tiny thing against so many bricks, then it is I look at trees. When there is nothing left to look at on this street. Four who grew despite concrete. Four who reach and do not forget to reach. Four whose only reason is to be and be." She understands that power can come from beauty, but that she "is the ugly daughter." Instead, Esperanza decides to be more like a man. "I have begun my own quiet war. Simple. Sure. I am the one who leaves the table like a man, without putting back the chair or picking up the plate." Thus, she refuses to take on the role of the victimized woman and maintains a sense of her own power.

Esperanza's intelligence and her ability to tell stories are what will ultimately free her from her current situation. Her mother blames the state of her own life on the fact that she did not get an education. Though she is a gifted singer and artist, she spends her days in the kitchen. She needs Esperanza's help to take the train downtown. "Shame is a bad thing, you know. It keeps you down. You want to know why I quit school? Because I didn't have nice clothes. No clothes, but I had brains. Yup, she says disgusted, stirring again. I was a smart cookie then."

The act of leaving the poor neighborhood in which she grew up, however, will not sever Esperanza's ties to her family and her origins. Just as her mother says, "got to take care all your own," so, too, must Esperanza return to Mango Street to rescue those who are unable to help themselves. When three sisters arrive mysteriously in the wake of a child's death, their parallel to the three witches of Shakespeare's *Macbeth* is inescapable. These women, who "did not seem to be related to anything but the moon," are soon enough telling Esperanza's fortune and granting her a wish. But it comes with a condition. "When you leave you must remember to come back for the others. A circle, understand? You will always be Esperanza. You will always be Mango street. You can't erase what you know. You can't forget who you are." It is this fierce desire to leave, the "hope" that Esperanza represents, that drives the novel.

Dysfunctional Gender Roles

Another recurrent theme in the novel is the dysfunctional gender roles in the community. Almost all the women Esperanza refers to are abused, afraid, and beaten down both emotionally and physically. They are locked inside the house, some bearing the signs of domestic abuse, and all forced to work or provide for their families on the most limited of means. Esperanza's models, such as they are, are women who have no hope or pride. Cisneros dedicates the book "A las mujeres" or "To the women" to emphasize that she is giving Hispanic women a voice.

When the reader begins to suspect that Esperanza's account of men in the novel is biased and unjustifiably harsh, Cisneros presents scenes from Esperanza's father's life. In the chapter called "Papa Who Wakes up Tired in the Dark," we understand why Esperanza's father is mostly absent from her narrative. He has "thick hands and thick shoes," and he "wakes up tired in the dark . . . combs his hair with water, drinks his coffee and is gone before we wake." He is obviously working hard for his family. When he comes into Esperanza's room to tell her that her grandfather has passed away, he "crumples like a coat and cries, my brave Papa cries. I have never seen my Papa cry and don't know what to do." His vulnerability simultaneously scares her and gives her an appreciation for all he has sacrificed for his family.

An understanding of adult activities and mistakes is one of the lessons Esperanza learns in the book. Esperanza gradually comes to understand her parents and the nature and mysteries of adult relationships and interactions. When she first questions why anyone would get married or let her husband treat her badly, she is sympathetic when her friend Sally marries young in order to escape her father. Additionally, through her sexual assault, she is also forcibly and violently ushered into the adult knowledge and awareness of sexuality. Unsurprisingly, it is an introduction that scars her. "You're a liar. They all lied. All the books and magazines, everything that told it wrong."

The Power of Words

The enduring image in the book is the power of words to express, catalog, bear witness, and to offer an escape. "I put it down on paper and then the ghost does not ache so much." When Minerva has given her children their meager dinners she "writes poems on little pieces of paper that she folds over and over and holds in her hands a long time." Writing for Minerva has the same cathartic effect; it allows her to continue living, just as writing will be Esperanza's salvation as well. Her vision of her future includes a departure that comes only after she has gathered the valuable objects she will take with her. "One day I will pack my bags of books and paper. One day I will say goodbye to Mango." Esperanza's words are what will save her.

CRISTINA GARCÍA

Biography

DRAWING ON HER intimate knowledge of Cuban culture and the expatriate communities of New York and Miami, Cristina García has emerged as one of North America's preeminent Cuban-American writers. García was born in Havana, Cuba, on July 4, 1958. Her father owned a cattle ranch and participated in the exodus of middle- and upper-class Cubans to the United States after Fidel Castro confiscated their ranches. In 1960, the family moved to New York and opened a restaurant. García worked there throughout her childhood and while attending Barnard College. She graduated in 1979 and went on to the Johns Hopkins University School of Advanced International Studies, graduating with a master's degree in European and Latin American studies in 1981 and intending to enter the foreign service.

Her flair for writing, however, took her down a different path, and García became a successful reporter and researcher. She held several internships during college and, after graduate school, worked for *Time* magazine where she climbed the ranks, becoming the San Francisco correspondent and then serving as the bureau chief in Miami after that. By 1990, she was writing fiction full time. Though she had always considered herself Cuban, it was her time in Miami that reawakened her interest in her Cuban roots and her family's history. In 1984, she returned to Cuba for the first time since she left at the age of two. She visited with many relatives, some of whom she had never met, likening the experience to "finding a missing link in my own identity." For five years, she wrestled with the strong emotions generated by the trip and, in 1989, began to write *Dreaming in Cuban*.

The novel was published three years later to tremendous critical praise, earning a National Book Award nomination. García gave birth to her daughter soon after the book's release; focused on being a new mother, she was surprised by the novel's reception and growing popularity in the ensuing years. Her second book, *The Agüero Sisters,* was inspired by her aunt's visit to her mother in Miami, which ended in a long estrangement. The novel came out in 1997 and won the Janet Heidinger Kafka Prize.

Despite the literary approval, García has weathered some criticism from Cubans. She is a part of the generation whose members, though born in Cuba and Spanish speaking, have lived the majority of their lives in the United States and who often view themselves as neither Cuban nor American. Some readers criticize her for the lack of political commentary in her novels, while some Cubans prefer she write in Spanish or claim that her experience does not represent theirs. García counters these arguments by saying that she is trying to express her version of the Cuban experience for English speakers and that "there is no one Cuban exile."

Her other works include *Monkey Hunting* (2003) and *Handbook to Luck* (2007), which won the Northern California Book Award. She has also edited two anthologies of Cuban and Hispanic literature. She is the recipient of a Whiting Award and has taught at various schools and universities throughout California. Currently, she lives in Northern California with her daughter and is a visiting professor at Mills College.

Dreaming in Cuban
Summary and Analysis

Dreaming in Cuban is a novel in three sections. Reflecting this triad theme, the book tells of three generations of Cuban women. Each section has several female voices that relate the story in the form of first-person narratives, third-person observances, and letters. In the first section, "Ordinary Seductions, 1972," the reader is introduced to the matriarch of the family, Celia del Pino. She keeps watch over the Cuban coastline, looking for American invaders. From her description, the reader is able to glean two facts: The main character is devoted to the Cuban revolutionary cause, and her grasp of reality is tenuous. She sees her husband walking up the beach toward her. As he is actually in New York getting cancer treatment, she concludes he must be dead. She is so used to him being away that she cannot grieve but goes into the water after him instead.

Felicia del Pino, Celia's daughter, is introduced. She has heard from her sister, Lourdes, that her father has died. The nuns who were caring for him told her he "rose to heaven on tongues of fire." Felicia goes with her friend Herminia to perform a Santería ritual that will cleanse her soul of her father's ghost. Meanwhile, in Brooklyn, Lourdes hears the nun's account of her father's ascension to heaven. She is the only member of the family who grieves. Upset at the news, she makes the wrong change and mixes up orders at the bakery she owns. She calls her husband, Rufino, for help, but he does not answer the phone; neither does her rebellious 13-year-old daughter, Pilar. When she comes home, she finds Pilar has run away.

Pilar had been walking down the street in Brooklyn when she saw her father kissing and walking arm in arm with a woman who was not her mother. Pilar takes all her money out of the bank and decides to go back to Cuba, to her grandmother Celia, with whom she has always had a close connection. She takes a bus to Florida with the intention of catching a boat when she gets there. While she rides, she explains that as a baby her caregivers considered her a witch. She remembers everything since the day she was born. She also tells of her grandfather's last days before her mother, Lourdes, consigned him to the nuns' care.

While Celia waits to pick up her twin granddaughters—Felicia's daughters—she remembers the first days of her marriage. She had been in love with a Spaniard, who left her to return to his home country. She then married Jorge, continuing to write to her Spaniard, though she never sent the letters. Her marriage to Jorge was unhappy. They lived with his mother and sister, who mistreated Celia. Anxious, Celia joined a volunteer work brigade, until an altercation between the sugarcane workers and the volunteers ended that pursuit. She returned home to find Felicia's mental state deteriorated and attempted to take the twins and Felicia's son, Ivanito, away, but the little boy refused to go. In a series of Celia's letters to the Spaniard from 1935 to 1940, it is revealed that Celia has a history of mental illness as well. She spent time in a mental hospital between the births of her daughters.

Pilar arrives in Florida and decides to look up one of her cousins. She finds him occupied in a house filled with her relatives and so curls up on a lawn chair to wait. She falls asleep and is discovered by her aunt who will tell Pilar's mother she has run away. She will have to return to Brooklyn, where Lourdes, on her way home from the bakery after firing one of her workers for stealing 50 cents, sees her father's ghost. He tells her that he will return from time to time. Lourdes then recalls traveling to the United States to join her husband and his family. Pilar, a little girl then, ran away at the airport. This memory leads to a darker one—while two months pregnant with her second child, Lourdes was bucked by a horse as she rode home to find soldiers threatening her husband at gunpoint. She yelled at them, "Get the hell out of here!" Though, surprisingly, they flee, afterward, she miscarries.

A still darker memory returns. The soldiers come back when her husband is away in Havana. This time, not put off by her screams, they rape and beat her, carving illegible letters into the flesh of her stomach.

Felicia becomes delusional and remembers how she and her sailor husband met. Working as a waitress, they exchanged few words before getting a hotel room. He left the next day, and when he returned, Felicia was seven months pregnant. Her father makes them marry, but her new husband tells her he will kill her if she tries to touch him. He returns to her one more time, infecting her with syphilis and impregnating her with Ivanito. This time, Felicia loses her grip on sanity and tries to kill him, throwing an oil-soaked rag in his face. As she descends into mental instability and illness, she grows more and more attached to her young son.

This bond could not be more different from the neglect that afflicted the previous generations of Celia's family. She was raised, after her mother abandoned her in the wake of her parents' divorce, by her aunt, an irreligious, independent woman. Celia cursed Lourdes whiles she was pregnant with her, and today Lourdes is barely on speaking terms with her mother, perpetuating the cycle of misunderstanding. Felicia, meanwhile, tries to kill herself, and Celia is awakened at the beach by a premonition. Celia's letters to the Spaniard, written between 1942 and 1949, tell of her son Javier's birth and a recognition of the suffering she feels is part of life.

The novel's second section, "Imagining Winter," takes place two years later. Felicia has joined a volunteer army, after her suicide attempt labeled her an "unfit mother" and her children were sent to boarding school. She does not fit in with the rest of the troops, however, and it is obvious that her mental health is still fragile.

One year later, Celia is serving on the community court, judging an adultery case. It depresses her that the seriousness of the court has been turned into a sideshow soap opera. She feels lonely and laments the loss of her connection with Pilar, her granddaughter.

Luz, one of Felicia's twin daughters, then tells how she and her sister reconnected with their father, whose scarred face keeps him out of society. They visit him in his hotel, and he buys them gifts. One day, they bring their little brother to see their father and catch him with a prostitute. Their little brother worries that his mother will find out.

In Brooklyn, mirroring her mother's revolutionary guard activities, Lourdes has become an auxiliary policewoman. She remains ardently anticommunist and anti-Castro, feeling that he stole the ranch she had worked so hard to make profitable. The family, once well off in Cuba, is now part of the working poor. Her husband, not cut out for indoor work, spends his time inventing useless items.

Pilar passes her time in clubs, listening to Lou Reed and punk rock. She also likes to paint. Her mother asks her to paint a picture for the bakery party in honor of America's bicentennial in 1976, and Pilar does, producing an image of a punk Statue of Liberty with a safety pin through her nose and being bombarded by bugs. Her mother is horrified when it is unveiled in public, but when someone criticizes it, she defends the painting, because it is her daughter's. Pilar gains new appreciation for her mother.

Felicia remarries impetuously, after meeting a man who had crashed his bicycle. Before he can even move in, though, he dies in a restaurant fire. She suspects that a spy in her beauty salon arranged the murder. She lures in the supposed mastermind and gives her a permanent with lye designed to cause great pain.

She then finds herself waking in an unfamiliar room. Naked, she puts on work clothes she sees lying on the floor and wanders out into the strange streets, where everyone seems to know her. She is claimed by a man who says he is her husband. Over the next week, she begins to remember her past. They ride on a Ferris wheel after the amusement park closes, and when he makes unwanted sexual advances, she pushes him off the ride to his death.

Celia's son Javier returns home from his exile in Czechoslovakia after his wife leaves him, taking their daughter. He retreats into alcohol abuse. Celia, desperate to help him, visits a *santera* who dissolves into dust just as Celia finds her. When she returns, Javier is gone. He joins the ranks of the absent: Lourdes, in Brooklyn; Pilar, with whom Celia has lost her connection; Felicia, who has disappeared; and the twins and Ivanito, far away at boarding school. The following week, Celia has a mastectomy when she discovers a cancerous lump.

Celia's letters to the Spaniard from 1950 to 1955 are filled with more worldly concerns. She speaks excitedly of the fomenting revolution, as she is anxious to get rid of then-president Fulgencio Batista. She also worries about and is proud of her children, fretting over Lourdes's coldness. Lourdes goes on a starvation diet and loses 118 pounds in a matter of months. Though her father's ghost worries about her, she insists she is fine. She grows paranoid, thinking that the communists are threatening the United States, and allows anti-Castro forces to meet in her bakery. She and Pilar are on no better terms. When she calls and Pilar does not answer her dormitory phone, Lourdes accuses her daughter of being a prostitute.

Pilar, meanwhile, has grown up, attending Barnard College and studying anthropology while painting constantly. Her Peruvian boyfriend cheats on her; to help alleviate her grief, she buys a bass guitar, teaching herself to play. Felicia returns from her mysterious disappearance and devotes herself to Santería, becoming a santera. Instead of curing her, though, her religious practices seem to make her weaker and more fragile. She stops eating and loses all her hair. Celia comes to care for her daughter, but there is nothing she can do, and Felicia dies.

The ghost of Lourdes's father appears less frequently but finally explains to her that her mother loved her but was pushed to the breaking point by his extended family. He tells Lourdes that he took her away from her mother, also revealing that her sister Felicia has died. He says she must go back to Cuba, but she refuses. He tells her he knows about her rape, though her mother does not. He begs her to return to Cuba to tell Celia that he is sorry.

Pilar visits a *botánica,* a store selling Santería-related herbs and items, where a man recognizes her as the daughter of the fire god Changó and entreats her to perform a ritual with herbs and baths. Pilar follows his instructions, and on the ninth day of bathing with herbs, she calls Lourdes and tells her that both of them are going to Cuba.

Celia's letters to the Spaniard from 1956 to 1958 tell of her sympathies for the revolutionary forces and her recognition that she loves her husband. She likes Lourdes's fiancé, though his mother is a disagreeable person who says that Celia's plans for a beach barbeque for the wedding reception are too tacky. Instead, the fiancé's mother plans and pays for a French dinner at an exclusive club, making Celia feel gauche and unsophisticated. Still, she is happy, she tells her Spaniard—she is going to be a grandmother.

Section 3 is titled "The Languages Lost" and is set in 1980. Celia buries her daughter Felicia. Pilar and her mother, Lourdes, arrive in Cuba amid civil unrest: "[A] busload of people seeking asylum crashed the gates of the Peruvian embassy." Pilar is fascinated by Cuba: "My mother and I pass billboards advertising the revolution as if it were a new brand of cigarette." They arrive to find Celia in a kind of trance, wearing Felicia's bathing suit. They give her a bath, leaving in the pearl drop earrings she never removes. Then Lourdes and Pilar go for a walk. Lourdes rants about the poor quality of the Russian cars and the slavish devotion to Castro. "They can't understand a word I'm saying! Their heads are filled with too much compañero [comrade] this and compañera that!" Pilar silences her mother's rant, noticing that "the language she speaks is lost to them. It's another idiom entirely."

Celia begins to tell Pilar about her life, and Lourdes returns to the ranch, where she is reminded of her miscarriage and rape. Everything seems decayed to her. Pilar paints Celia. Lourdes arranges for Ivanito to seek asylum, writing him to say she will sponsor him and dropping him off at the Peruvian embassy. Celia gives Pilar the letters that she wrote but never sent to the Spaniard, and Pilar begins to dream in Spanish. She loves Cuba but realizes it is not her home. Celia walks into the ocean. She takes off her earrings, dropping each into the ocean. She "imagines it drifting as a firefly through the darkened seas, imagines its slow extinguishing." The last page of the novel is a letter from Celia to the Spaniard dated 1959. She says that the revolution has begun and that her granddaughter Pilar was just born, on the same day as Celia's birthday. She says she will no longer write because Pilar "will remember everything" proving the letters to be, not love letters, but a record of Celia's life, now over.

Major Themes

García uses many different narrators in the novel in order to give voice to and represent the various and diverse aspects of Cuban experience. Though she does not claim to speak for everyone, by describing various individual struggles—for mental health, acceptance, love, recovery, and connection—she gives voice to Cuban women and the range of challenges they faced.

The Power of Memory

García's book is concerned with the various ways memory affects and influences the present. This theme is conveyed and developed in a variety of ways in the novel. First, García herself can be seen as creating a record of the Cuban experience in English. So, in the act of writing the novel, she is creating memories of Cuba for English speakers, imparting a sort of history lesson. Then, there are Celia's letters. At the end of the novel, it is revealed that she stops writing when Pilar is born, because Pilar will serve as Celia's living memory. Therefore, the letters are not the love letters they initially seem to be but a diary or record of that period in Celia's, and by extension Cuba's, life. Third, Pilar serves as a recording device. She has a gift for communicating with her grandmother wordlessly, across bodies of water. She also remembers everything from the day she was born in great detail. This leads her early caregivers to dismiss her as a witch, but it also makes her a living record, the perfect vessel for describing and remembering the forgotten ones in Cuba. Her profession as a painter underscores that role; Pilar paints Celia and other images, recording them for posterity.

Rebellion and Revolution

Revolution is another central theme in García's book. All three generations of women are obsessed with rebellion. Celia is a devotee of Castro. She volunteers as a worker, judge, and lookout. She never admits that Cuba is anything other than better off since the revolution and tries to get Felicia to join the cause as a way of improving her mental health. Celia's other daughter, Lourdes, meanwhile, is obsessed with denouncing the revolution. She has not been back to Cuba since she emigrated, and she allows her bakery to become a meeting place for anti-Castro activists. She is so devoted to making money that she ignores her husband and daughter, obsessively eating the pastries as a replacement for their love and affection. Like her mother's aid to the forces in Cuba, she volunteers for the auxiliary police. The parallels between the two women, futilely trying to stave off violence by keeping watch in the evenings, is obvious. When Lourdes decides to lose weight, she eats nothing until she is at the weight she desires. For her, it is all or nothing.

Pilar's rebellion is less radical and more expected from a teenager. She despises her mother, is embarrassed by how out of touch Lourdes is, and expresses herself through painting and punk rock music. When she paints the portrait of the Statue of Liberty with a safety pin through her nose, she is rebelling against not only her mother, whom she knows will be embarrassed and angry by the painting, but also her adopted country. She is saying simultaneously that she does not respect the traditional symbol of American immigrants and that she has made the United States her own by transforming, through her own artistic vision, one of its key national symbols.

Still, Pilar longs for the homeland she does not remember. She runs away to try to find her grandmother, with whom she shares a kindred spirit, but does not make it back to Cuba until she and her mother travel there at the end of the novel. Pilar discovers that, while she does not feel totally at home in the United States, it is more her home than Cuba is, with its restrictions on expression and its decaying infrastructure.

Depression and Mental Illness

The del Pino women have a history of mental illness. First Celia and then Felicia spend time in mental health facilities where they do not receive adequate treatment. Celia, driven to the brink of sanity by her in-laws, is denied the rest she needs, while Felicia is released without being cured and goes on to injure her first husband and murder her third. Lourdes, while a functional woman, still bears literal and figurative scars from the assault and miscarriage she endured before emigrating. Mental illness in the novel emerges as the only way for the women to express their unhappiness in the highly restrictive society in which they live. Unfortunately, the legacy of the illness extends to the younger generation, as Ivanito's childhood is stunted by his mother, Felicia's, illness.

Religion, Spirituality, and the Supernatural

Cuba is a secular society, so the women do not have organized religion to turn to. Celia treats the revolution like a religion, with fanatical devotion. Lourdes turns to food, while Felicia embraces Santería, the religion that evolved from Yoruban, Catholic, and Native American rituals. Felicia is devoted enough to be ordained as a priestess, even though that cannot save her from her doomed fate. Celia and Felicia accept, however, the existence of the supernatural. Lourdes is unsurprised to see her father's ghost appear and talks with him as though he is another living character in the book. For good or bad, the connections between the generations are not severed, not even by death.

ERNESTO QUIÑONEZ

Biography

ERNESTO QUIÑONEZ was born in 1966 in Ecuador. His family of seven moved to East Harlem in New York City when Quiñonez was 18 months old. His father, a communist librarian and a strong influence on the young Ernesto, was threatened after an anti-communist coup. Equally as influential to the young boy was his mother, a devout Puerto Rican Jehovah's Witness. Ethnicity and religion are central to Quiñonez's conception of the Hispanic community.

The family was poor. For 20 years, Quiñonez's mother worked in the garment district in what the author describes as a sweatshop, "pushing pedals for Mr. Singer." His father was a factory worker, until a work-related injury forced the family to go on welfare for two years. They lived in the projects. In junior high, Quiñonez made pocket money by painting death-themed RIP (rest in peace) murals, like the autobiographical Chino in *Bodega Dreams*. He went on to become a teacher in a bilingual classroom of fourth graders and fought to give them the same privileges and opportunities, such as exposure to art classes and computers, afforded the gifted and talented students.

Quiñonez began to write after hearing a lecture by Frederic Tuten, who had been a teacher of Oscar Hijuelos. Walter Mosley became his mentor at the City College creative writing program. Quiñonez cites his literary influences as the Nuyorican (Puerto Rican-New York) poets he read in high school: Lucky Cienfuegos, Pedro Pietri, Piri Thomas, Sandra Maria Estevez, Shorty Bon Bon, Miguel Algarin, and Miguel Piñero to name a few. He equates the growth and development of Hispanic-American literature to the rise of the Jewish novel in the 1950s and 1960s, as his and other writers' novels are increasingly read, taught, and integrated into the canon of literature.

As a child, the Young Lords, the Hispanic activist group, was a major presence in Quiñonez's neighborhood. The New York branch of the Chicago-born organization acted as stewards of the community. They created a free breakfast program for children, organized clothing drives, set up free health clinics, and sponsored cultural festivals and Puerto Rican history classes. They also pushed for prisoner rehabilitation, Vietnam veterans' benefits, and women's rights. They served as crossing guards, community activists, and became members of local community boards. "They seemed strong and good to me then," he says. They are prominently featured in his first book not only because the main character, Willie Bodega, is a former Lord but also because Quiñonez wants to make sure they are not forgotten. "They are part of our national lore, just like American cowboys." With Quiñonez's debut novel, *Bodega Dreams,* their legacy is honored and perpetuated.

Bodega Dreams
Summary and Analysis

The chapters in *Bodega Dreams* are organized like a boxing match—there are three bouts. Each chapter serves as a round—the last one is a knockout—followed by a eulogy. In the first chapter Sapo, Spanish for "toad," is introduced. He is the narrator's friend from childhood who "did look like a toad" and who liked to bite when he was in fights. The reader also gets to know the neighborhood of Spanish Harlem in northern Manhattan. In Quiñonez's eyes, it is a tight-knit, poor, violent community where many men feel they must prove themselves to get respect. One sign of this respect is the bestowing of a nickname. The narrator is called Chino, because of his indigenous appearance and the Ecuadorian heritage he brings to his all-Puerto Rican neighborhood. Blanca, whose real name is Nancy, is also introduced. She is called "white" because of her devotion to her Pentecostal church (and in contrast to her sister, Negra). The narrator reveals his crush on Blanca. His junior high school is filled with delinquents and troublemakers, and the white teachers only serve to reinforce the students' low self-esteem. Hispanic teachers try to make a difference, but they do not have enough seniority or power to change the system. Throughout his childhood, Chino has no idea that his school is named Julia de Burgos, after Puerto Rico's most famous poet.

Round 2 finds the grown narrator attending college and expecting a baby with Blanca, now his wife. Both place a high value on their education and work full time while putting themselves through school. The neighborhood, though they have not left it, "became less important." Together, the newlyweds work hard "to invent new people . . . that's what it was always about. Shedding your past. Creating yourself from nothing."

Blanca and Chino frequently fight over his friendship with Sapo. Blanca thinks he is a bad influence on her husband, since he deals drugs and occasionally asks to store his supply in Chino and Blanca's apartment. One day, Sapo asks Chino to take the drug stash and give it to a mutual acquaintance. Chino does Sapo the favor, and Sapo gives him $50, telling him that Willie Bodega wants to see him.

In round 3 of the novel, at one of Willie Bodega's crash pads, Chino and Sapo meet Nene, the mysterious Bodega's cousin. Large and described as a little "slow," Nene speaks almost exclusively in lyrics from 1980s music. Bodega is revealed to be "a man in his forties with a goatee and the droopy eyes of an ex-heroin addict." Bodega begins to speak to Chino about his dream for East Harlem and the Puerto Rican people. As far as he is concerned, using crime to get to the top is a viable plan. "B'cause men that made this country, men that built this country were men from the street. . . . Men that used whatever money makin' scheme they could, and made enough money to clean their names by sending their kids to Harvard." Bodega sells drugs to buy old tenements, renovating them and offering the apartments to families at reduced rents. These families, he believes, will protect him by rioting if he is ever jailed. Additional protection comes in the form of Edwin Nazario, Bodega's lawyer.

Bodega dreams of completing the revolution started by the Young Lords in the late 1970s, a movement centered on Puerto Rican nationalism and pride. "Willie Bodega don't sell rocks. Willie Bodega sells dreams." When the two friends leave, Sapo is angry that Chino did not give Bodega a chance. He explains the real reason Bodega wants to get close to Chino: Blanca's cousin Vera. Vera was in love with Bodega but married a rich Cuban on the advice of her mother. Chino realizes that Bodega's talk of equality and power is motivated by his desire to impress Vera.

That night, Blanca tells Chino about the special guest speaker coming to her church, an "anointed one" who has been chosen as a spiritual leader at only 17 years of age. But Chino is not listening, thinking instead of how easy it would be to arrange for Bodega to become reacquainted with Vera and that, in exchange, Chino and Blanca could have a cheaper, bigger apartment, with a room for the new baby. He only has to tell Bodega that he will join his business operation.

Chino goes to Negra's apartment to ask about Vera. He finds Negra and her husband, Victor, in the aftermath of a fight. After suspecting that Victor had been unfaithful, she stabbed him with a kitchen knife. Victor whispers that he does not want to go to the nearby hospital because his girlfriend works there. Later, Negra tells Chino that Vera is planning a visit to New York.

Chino arrives home to an angry Blanca. Willie Bodega's apartment has come through, and Blanca has found a lease under the door. This reopens a longstanding conflict over Chino concealing the truth of his activities to his wife. He is able to assuage her anger, though, after promising to help look for a husband for Blanca's church friend Claudia, an illegal immigrant who wants to remain in the United States.

Bodega calls for Chino again, and Chino overhears him discussing a man named Alberto Salazar with Edwin Nazario, Bodega's lawyer. Chino tells Bodega that Vera is coming to New York, to be honored by a school, which is naming its auditorium after her. Later, Bodega summons Chino to the Museo del Barrio, a museum of Hispanic-American history. Though the museum is not yet open, it is a sign of Bodega's power and standing in the community that, when Chino says he has come to meet the powerful Bodega, the guard lets him in immediately. Bodega opens up to Chino and tells him about his experience with the Young Lords. Vera loved him, he says, and she did not mind his financial instability. She worried, though, that he had no vision of how to earn money. Now, Bodega tells Chino, he has both money and vision, and he expects that she will leave her husband and marry him.

As Chino and Blanca prepare to move into their new apartment, Chino sees on television that a reporter for a small Spanish-language paper has been found dead. His name was Alberto Salazar, and he had been investigating drug lords in East Harlem. Plus, he was found with a large bite out of his left shoulder.

Book 2 opens with the same first paragraph as book 1, only now the mention of Sapo's "reputation for biting" leads Chino to suspect that Sapo killed the reporter. Walking to work one day, Chino sees Nazario, dressed in a suit, holding court in the neighborhood like an especially popular politician. Bodega hands out favors through Nazario, helping recently arrived immigrants find jobs, paying tuition for private schools, and extending loans to start small businesses. In exchange for his kindness and assistance, he only asks that people remember that it was Bodega who helped them out. Nazario suggests that Chino come to meet Vera at the school naming its auditorium after her. Chino insists he has to work, but when he gets to his job, his boss tells him that he should go home, hinting that Nazario has arranged for this unexpected day off.

Nazario walks Chino back to his apartment to change, and on the way stops at a small museum that Chino did not know existed: the museum of salsa. The curator's daughter has just graduated from medical school, financed by "the program," as Nazario calls Bodega's investment in the future of East Harlem. The museum fills Chino with pride, and he begins to imagine that Bodega's dream is perhaps possible.

Bodega waits for Chino at his apartment, pacing and worrying like a teenager in love. When they get to the school, Bodega suddenly tries to back out of meeting Vera. Chino talks him into staying. When the ceremony starts, though, Chino realizes he has been used. Bodega could have easily found Vera on his own. He also most likely put up the money that got the school to dedicate the auditorium to Vera in order to lure her to New York. Chino feels manipulated but then realizes that Bodega wanted Chino involved in his business ventures because he and Blanca are family. Chino debates going to the police or confessing his involvement to Blanca, but he knows she will want to move out of their spacious new apartment. Although Chino notes that "with Bodega all you can hope for is that the good outweighs the bad," he still confronts Bodega with a direct question: "Why'd you have Salazar killed?"

Bodega explains that Salazar was a shady journalist working for Bodega's rival, Aaron Fischman, who is attempting to claim some of Bodega's drug territory. Sapo did not commit the actual murder, he adds. Vera and Bodega's reunion goes well; they show up at Chino's apartment in the early morning hours, drunk on champagne. Vera gives Chino her engagement ring. Blanca and Chino fight about keeping the ring, then continue arguing about Blanca's Pentecostalism, before moving on to Chino's involvement with Bodega. Chino realizes that if Blanca finds out the extent of his involvement with Bodega, she will leave him.

To make up with his wife, Chino attends a Pentecostal service at which the young anointed leader, Roberto Vega, is speaking. He whips the crowd into a religious frenzy, and Chino appreciates his power, wishing he had faith like those in the congregation. After the service, Blanca invites the pastor, her friend Claudia, and Roberto Vega and his family for dinner. On the way home, a neighbor informs them that their apartment building is on fire. When Chino sees Nazario emerging from the burning building, he realizes that Fischman had set the fire in retaliation for Salazar's death. "The war," he notes, "was in full bloom."

Nazario arranges for Blanca and Chino to move into another apartment. Chino goes into the flooded building and manages to retrieve the package he was storing for Sapo as well as the ring that Vera had given him. In the middle of the move, Sapo takes Chino to meet Nazario, who has him change into a suit and drives him to Queens. They speak to an old Italian man, a Mafia boss, to ask if he has any objection to Bodega putting Fischman out of business. The old man says he is retired, and he does not care who comes out on top. Chino thinks the talk goes well, but Nazario is fuming, humiliated by asking for a favor.

At home, Chino finds Blanca talking to Roberto and Claudia. They are in love and, despite their 10-year age difference, want to get married. Blanca thinks that Roberto needs to tell his mother, but Chino says they should just elope. He thinks of offering them the diamond ring. Bodega summons Chino and informs him that Vera's husband is coming to town the following day. He wants Chino and Blanca there when Vera confronts him and asks for a divorce. Chino gives him back the ring and considers his conflicted feelings about Bodega. "Whatever evil deed had been committed, something good was coming out of it. . . . Someone had to step forward and do something. Bodega had, because no one but one of its own residents was going to improve Spanish Harlem. No one."

The next evening, two detectives, DeJesus and Ortiz, come to ask Chino questions about Salazar's death. Blanca is horrified by the development and goes to her mother's house. At the police station, Chino gets into a heated verbal exchange with DeJesus, who expresses disdain because Chino "smell[s] like Boricua," adding "[i]f it was up to me I'd send you all back to that monkey island of yours." The captain questions Chino, who denies all knowledge of Bodega. As they let him go, Detective Ortiz takes Chino aside and apologizes for his partner's insults, explaining that he, Ortiz, is also Puerto Rican but that he has to support his partner.

The following day, Sapo tells Chino to meet Vera, Bodega, and Vera's husband at a restaurant. Vera tells her spouse she does not love him, but her husband begs her to come back, explaining to everyone that Vera has been unfaithful many times in the past. The discussion dissolves into a fight, and Vera suddenly shoots her husband. Bodega immediately volunteers to take the blame for the murder, but by the next day, Chino reveals, Bodega is dead. as Chino is informed of that fact when the detectives return, this time to question him about Bodega's murder. Chino gets to the station to find Nazario already there. Nazario advises him to deny that he was at the restaurant where Vera's husband was shot. Nazario reveals that Bodega was shot by Fischman's people on his way to turn himself in for the murder. The lawyer convinces Chino that it is better for Bodega to take the blame for the murder, since he is dead already. Negra and Blanca come to see Chino, revealing that Vera had had many affairs but that the man she loved was named Nazario. "It was all falling into place," Chino thinks. As Negra says, addressing her brother-in-law by his given name: "You, Julio . . . have been played."

Book 3 relates the results of Vera and Nazario's plot to murder Bodega. Chino goes in search of Sapo—who is lying low, planning to take over Bodega's empire—before informing the police. The entire neighborhood attends the funeral. Contrary to what Bodega predicted, no one riots to avenge his death. Instead, the neighborhood mourns him quietly. Many of the Young Lords with whom Bodega had demonstrated attend the funeral. Chino confronts Nazario about his role in killing Bodega. "I know everything. . . . You betrayed all those beautiful things." Then the police come to arrest him and Vera.

On his way home, Chino is asked by an old man and his son where they can find Bodega, who had promised to help them find jobs and shelter. Chino takes pity on them and invites them to stay in his apartment, since Blanca is now living at her mother's. That night Chino dreams that Bodega comes to his door, dressed as a Young Lord, with a copy of a protest magazine under his arm. They go on the fire escape and listen as a woman calls to her son in Spanglish. Bodega tells him, "What we just heard was a poem, Chino. It's a beautiful new language." Chino looks down at East Harlem. "Bodega was right, it was alive. Its music and people had taken off their mourning clothes. The neighborhood had turned into a maraca, with the men and women transformed into sees, shaking with love and desire for one another." Chino contemplates Bodega's legacy: "The way a picture that's been hanging on a wall for years leaves a shadow of light behind, Bodega had kicked the door down and left a green light of hope for everyone. He had represented the limitless possibilities in us all by living his life, striving for those dreams. . . . Tomorrow Spanish Harlem would run faster, fly higher, stretch its arms farther, and one day those dreams would carry its people to new beginnings."

Major Themes

Hispanic New York

Bodega Dreams is loosely based on two classics of literature: *The Catcher in the Rye* by J. D. Salinger and *The Great Gatsby* by F. Scott Fitzgerald. The influence of *The Catcher in the Rye* is perhaps the most obvious. The book begins with the line "How I grew up and all that other Piri Thomas kind of crap," an almost direct quote of Salinger's novel.

Gatsby makes his appearance in the form of Willie Bodega, a revered but flawed hero who is brought down because of his unrequited love for a married woman.

It is interesting that Quiñonez references these two novels, as they are classic representations of the privileged white New York experience. By using these two novels as a basis for his exploration of Spanish Harlem, he reclaims both New York and literature for Hispanic peoples.

Moral Ambiguity

Willie Bodega is a controversial character. He is a drug pusher who sells to other Puerto Ricans, but he is also a source of housing and neighborhood improvement in an area that government and law enforcement have neglected. Bodega, who takes his nickname from the small convenience stores that pepper Harlem, is a quintessentially Spanish Harlem product. He dreams big but feels that the only way to achieve these goals is through crime and force. Quiñonez says of his character: "I wanted to take on that question—of heroism, and the dark side of heroism, head on, and the way that seemed most relevant was through a figure like this. I wanted to invoke some ambivalence in the figure of a street hero, a hero who isn't just a hero, a villain who isn't a villain, to look at both sides of the coin, in the figure of one particular street lord, a guy who's getting older and is seeing his dreams starting to tarnish." Quiñonez achieves a complexity and a realism in his portrayal of Bodega, a man who uses criminal means to achieve positive, transformative goals.

The Effects of Violence

Quiñonez's novel has many examples of the violence that plagues the neighborhood. The book opens with the image of Sapo biting his opponents during fights. Quiñonez describes in detail the fights his main character has to endure in order to win the respect of his contemporaries. Chino's good friend Sapo may have committed murder; at the very least, he was present when the reporter was killed. Still, Chino defends him, even as he struggles to play by the rules.

Violence, in the form of domestic disturbance, fires, physical altercations, or murder is prominently featured in the novel. Quiñonez based the character of Sapo on a real friend of his, who fell off a roof when the boys were 14. The character is a tribute to his dead friend, as well as to others who did not survive the neighborhood.

Central to the novel is the question of engaging in violence. Julio continually struggles with maintaining his ties to the neighborhood while refraining from illegal activities. Yet he defends the violent actions of others. Quiñonez says one of the central questions he wants his characters to address is "Should I fight? How do I fight? Is there ever a just cause for violence?"

Cultural/Historical Legacies

Additionally, history plays a large role in the novel. Willie Bodega lives almost constantly in the past, longing for a time of activism and national pride that is no more.

He pines after a woman who left him years ago, and he attempts to re-create a drug empire reminiscent of the Mafia hold on Harlem in previous decades. The old Mafia boss Chino and Nazario visit praises Bodega for his old-fashioned ways.

One aspect of history that Quiñonez highlights is the pride and legacy of the Puerto Rican people. He explains that no one knew the poet after whom his school was named, Julia de Burgos. Few remember the Young Lords. These are aspects of the cultural heritage that must be preserved, according to the characters in the novel. Nazario brings Chino to the museum of salsa that Chino never knew existed, and Bodega meets him in the Museo del Barrio, where he comments on the legacy of Hispanic art that goes almost unrecognized.

It is no coincidence that the last section of the book is called "A New Language Being Born." In Quiñonez's opinion, Spanglish is not a mixture of English and Spanish but an entirely new language. In Chino's dream, the joy that Bodega takes at hearing the fluent Spanglish sentence suggests that this new language will be used to express a variety of hopes and dreams.

Chango's Fire
Summary and Analysis

Ernesto Quiñonez's second novel shares many elements with his first. Both protagonists are named Julio (though Chino goes by his nickname); both attend college at night; both make East Harlem their homes. Additionally, both are striving to rise above the cycle of poverty and violence that has plagued their neighborhoods.

Julio Santana is proud of what he has accomplished. What he is not proud of is the way he has achieved his goals. He has purchased the third story of a three-apartment building for him and his parents to live in, but he has financed it through arson. The local bigwig, an Italian named Eddie, runs an insurance fraud scheme, and Julio has been his protégé. Julio is good at setting fires, but most of all, he is good at resisting the temptation to steal from the houses he is burning.

One night a starving cat climbs into his open back window, and he decides to bring it home to his mother. As he stands in the entranceway, a white girl who has just moved into the building demands that he produce keys or ring the buzzer, because she is afraid to let in strangers. He is taken with her looks, but she offends him by complaining how much her apartment cost, "even in this neighborhood," and then further offends him by trying to repair the damage by asking him to coffee at Starbucks. To Julio, the coffee-serving chain store is a symbol of the gentrification taking place in his neighborhood. He is tired of the encroaching hipsters with their lounges and coffeehouses pushing up prices and changing the family-oriented nature of the blocks on which he grew up.

Julio's parents, though born in Puerto Rico, have made East Harlem their home. His mother is a devout Pentecostal, a form of Protestantism, who detests the idolatry of Catholicism and Santería. His father has a history of drug addiction and a gift for playing salsa music. He repeats constantly the stories of when he played with Hector Lavoe, one of the greatest salsa musicians.

Julio works a day job as part of a demolition crew. Eddie arranged for the job, and Julio is one of only two workers who speak English or have legal work permits. The other workers, mostly Mexican, have borrowed other people's names and social security numbers. On payday, they collect their checks and hand them to the white men who give them cash in exchange for a portion of the total amount. No one complains—the men are earning more than they would in their native country, and they are at risk for deportation. One worker, Mario, has recently been released from prison.

On Julio's way home from work, he drops his mortgage money off with Papelito. Papelito owns the local botanica, a center for Santería supplies. Papelito is a priest, and his store is always full of women looking for cures to get their straying husbands to come back or a way to discern the winning lottery numbers. Papelito is a gay man who is accepted by the residents of the neighborhood. He has done Julio a favor by putting his own name on the deed. Otherwise, a bank would not give Julio a loan, since most of his income, from arson, is undeclared. Julio stares up at his building with pride, even though he also sees its shabbiness and the much-needed repairs.

Julio then checks on his friend, Trompo Loco. Though his real name is Eduardo, everyone calls him "crazy top," because when he gets upset he spins himself into a frenzy. It is unclear exactly what Trompo's disability is, but Julio takes pity on him, since his naïve nature consistently gets him into trouble. In his latest scheme, Trompo has found a hard hat and is trying to convince Julio to let him come to the demolition site. Julio tries to convince him to stay away. The neighborhood's worst-kept secret is that Eddie is Trompo Loco's father, though he has never acknowledged his son. Trompo Loco, meanwhile, is desperately trying to fit in—to get a job, get his father to recognize him, and to live a normal life.

On the stairs, Julio meets up with Helen, the woman from the second floor, who is sobbing, her head in her hands. Julio tries to comfort her and tells her she can knock if she needs anything. Upstairs, his mother barely has time to tell him that the cat has fled through the fire escape, when the doorbell rings. Helen apologizes for not letting him in the building the other night. She says she is opening an art gallery and expresses her anger at how people have treated her in her new neighborhood. One woman yelled, "White bitch go home." Julio tries to explain to her the history of the neighborhood and the animosity between the different groups living there, but Helen shakes her head. "You still believe two wrongs make a right."

At the job site, the boss is upset because someone has stolen the expensive pipes. "I know it was one of yous," he accuses the Mexican workers, whom he degradingly calls "tacos." Julio's troubles, however, have just begun. He runs into Maritza, the pastor of a church that occupies the first floor of Julio's building. She insists that Julio drive her and a young woman to a clinic in Queens where the girl tearfully insists that she needs surgery to make her a virgin again. They only have $900, though, and the surgery costs $2,000, so Maritza begs Julio for the money. He agrees to the loan if she will hire Trompo Loco to help her clean the church and pay him the money instead.

Helen sends Julio a letter, explaining her anger the last time they spoke. "I have a weird blend of haughtiness and guilt" she says and admits to having romanticized her new neighborhood. Julio reads the letter multiple times; it is clear he is falling for her. He goes to see Papelito to ask him to read his *letra,* or fortune. Papelito explains that the Orishas (or the Santerían gods) say that no one has asked the gods to harm Julio, and that there are two women who will come into his life. One is white, and one is dark and will give him sons. Though Julio does not believe Papelito's words, he feels some hope that Helen might like him. Papelito gives him instructions: He must erect an altar to Ochun, the goddess of love and marriage, and buy five candles and five pastries and at the end of five days throw them into the East River. Julio asks him what makes his faith so strong, and he replies that Santería is like any other religion, a series of stories and rituals to live by. Julio considers the power of prayer and wonders if he might want to trade in Christianity for another religion.

Julio goes to pick up the money for his arson job and tells Eddie that he is quitting their venture. Eddie tries to convince him otherwise then asks about Julio's "friend," meaning Trompo Loco. Julio responds that Trompo thinks Eddie is his father. Eddie denies it but tells Julio to keep an eye on Trompo. Eddie then asks Julio for one more favor: A rich kid got a Lexus as a present and wants the insurance money instead. He hands Julio a set of keys and tells him to steal the car.

Julio runs into Helen as he is walking to the East River to throw the pastries in the water, per Papelito's instructions. She invites him into the gallery, and they share a drink, becoming increasingly intimate. Afterward, Julio dresses and leaves quickly. Julio is summoned back to Eddie's, who offers him a job in Washington, D.C., burning old buildings and sitting on them until the government awards money for their reconstruction. Julio refuses; he wants to finish school and wants to lead a crime-free life. Eddie then points to a black cat, which Julio recognizes as the one he brought home from the fire. When the animal escaped, it returned to the burned house it had lived in. The claims adjusters wonder how a cat could survive an electrical fire and entertain the notion that it was not an electrical fire after all. Eddie tells Julio that he owes him for the insurance and insists he take the job in Washington, D.C. When Julio refuses again, Eddie tells him his only other choice is to burn down his own building. Eddie does not know that the apartment is in Papelito's name.

In book 2, Julio's mother becomes suspicious when she goes to the bank to inquire about a home equity loan and they tell her that her son has no mortgage there. She confronts him, but Julio lies to her, telling her that their apartment is not such a great place anyway and that they might move soon. She sees his altar and gets angry at his idolatry, claiming that he has invited evil spirits into the house. Julio meets Helen for a drink at a lounge filled with new white arrivals to the neighborhood. He walks in and someone approaches him to ask him where to buy drugs. Julio says he does not know. Then, a Hispanic man comes up to Julio and tries to strike up a conversation, saying that he hates the fact that everyone assumes that all Hispanics deal drugs. He comes to the lounge, though, because it has a brand-new pool table. Thus, Julio is sandwiched between two stereotypes involving Hispanic identity and criminality. He finally sees Helen, who has been meeting with her business partner. He has bought a brownstone nearby and has received death threats in his mailbox. Julio and Helen leave together, but she takes offense at the catcalls she receives outside a deli and argues with the men who leered at her. When she refuses to back down, the men turn on Julio, and the pool player from the lounge comes out to calm the situation. Julio walkes the drunken and agitated Helen safely home and puts her to bed.

Julio's boss decides to dock his and all the other workers' pay for the stolen pipes. Ex-convict Mario says that everyone knows Julio owes Eddie money and asks if Eddie knows anything about a series of forms that someone in the neighborhood is selling. These forms give automatic citizenship to anyone who possesses one. Julio says he just wants his check, but when he sees the boss, he is told his wages have been garnished by Eddie. Maritza, Helen, and Julio then witness a group of women beating a man with broomsticks. The man has been molesting his daughter and has given both his wife and daughter AIDS. Helen comes by Julio's house. She is humiliated because she went to a community board meeting and no one wanted to discuss gentrification. She also says she admires Maritza, even though Julio laughs off her church as a mere platform for her personal politics. Visiting Helen's apartment, Julio tries to confess that he is an arsonist, but she does not take him seriously. He begins to think that "Helen has become another fact in my life."

After class one evening, Mario approaches Julio and calls him by his last name. Julio sees that the supposed ex-convict is actually a federal agent. Mario says he is not interested in Julio's arson activities nor in Eddie's insurance fraud, but rather in the lost citizenship forms he is certain Maritza is hiding in her church. Julio says he will try to investigate. At Maritza's church, he listens to a woman testify that her sister's husband had been cheating on her with another man. The sister has died of AIDS, and the woman was so humiliated that she was not able to tell the community what really happened. Julio looks at the faces of the recent, mostly illegal, immigrants in the audience and thinks that Maritza's message of AIDS activism is lost on them; they are only there to get the citizenship documents.

Helen sends Julio another letter drawing parallels between Spanish Harlem and her changing midwestern town and asking him to meet her at the Metropolitan Museum of Art where "the paintings . . . dream in color." His father reads the note and issues two warnings: First, he should not tell his mother that he is dating Helen, as she will get her hopes up and have them married off in her fantasy by the end of the week; second, he tells Julio that the neighborhood is constantly changing and that he should not be mad at newcomers who have every right to be there. "You can't be angry at her for not understanding."

Julio is invited to his co-worker Antonio's apartment, which he shares with eight other men. Antonio admits to having an affair with Maritza and says that he has not accepted a document granting him citizenship because he is proud to be Mexican. He also tells Julio that Maritza only gives documents to people who have AIDS. Julio tells Mario he has not been able to find out anything about the missing forms. Papelito begs Julio to confess his criminal activities to his mother. He also speaks of the ways of the spirits and explains more about how Santería works.

Julio tells Maritza that the government is after her. Papelito admits that he knows Mario's true identity. Papelito is hiding the documents for Maritza, who found them in a discarded file cabinet, but he resents that she is using them to draw people to her church. Eddie tells Julio that he has to burn his house down the following evening or Eddie will hire someone else, who may or may not warn his family, to do the deed.

The same night as Helen's gallery opening, Papelito decides to let a reporter film an *Asiento*, or a ritual initiation, which prevents Julio from warning Papelito about the fire. Julio goes to Helen's gallery where he meets her parents. He tells her that he will be setting fire to her apartment the following evening. She threatens to call the police, but at that moment Trompo Loco enters the gallery, spinning and saying he has set fire to Julio's building so that Eddie will then have to recognize him as his son. His spinning destroys the gallery. Julio runs back to the building where he sees his parents and the cat standing outside. Papelito, in the middle of his ceremony, had a vision and came to the apartment to get Julio's parents out. He died in the fire, and Julio's mother declares him a saint.

Julio's family moves back to a housing project. Helen avoids Julio, though she has moved nearby. Julio goes to a santero to ask to be initiated into the religion. He is ready "to walk in the ways of the saints." The man initially refuses, but when he finds out that Julio was a friend of Papelito's and was known as a son of Changó—the god of fire and lightning—he agrees to teach him the ways of the religion. Helen stops by to ask Julio if he would like to go with her to hear the Dalai Lama speak, though she is only ready to see him in public places. Though he has returned to life in a housing project and has no job, Julio feels a glimmer of hope.

Major Themes

Gentrification and Change

One of the novel's central themes is the gentrification of Harlem. As people are pushed out of pricier areas because of rising rents, they move to less expensive neighborhoods. In Julio's neighborhood, this migration is a cause for alarm. Rents will rise, restaurants and bars that the locals cannot afford will appear, and, perhaps most significantly, the neighborhood as a tight-knit community will dissipate.

Helen emerges as the new face of change. Julio is conflicted. He is attracted to her and wants to learn more about her, but she represents the influx of outsiders that he resents. She arrives full of righteous hope, trying to open an art gallery, which is ambitious and perhaps misguided. She frequents the kinds of bars that Julio avoids. In short, she does not understand the neighborhood; she responds to catcalls with anger and direct confrontation, unaware of the violent repercussions her boldness may provoke. She is appalled by the lack of police protection and the unfair treatment of women. She even attends a community meeting and is outraged that no one will talk about the very gentrification that she represents. Still, she realizes that merely taking Spanish classes or attempting to understand the culture will not integrate her into her new world. She is a perennial outsider.

Julio's mother welcomes Helen; she wants Julio to marry Helen and produce blond grandchildren. However, it is Julio's father who intrusively reads Helen's two letters and who tries to reconcile Julio's conflicted feelings. The father explains that if Julio wants to show Helen the barrio he is so proud of, he needs to take her back to the East Harlem of the 1960s, when the activist movement and the neighborhood were at their peak. The old Spanish Harlem is no more, he believes, despite the fact that it was not too long ago that Puerto Rican newcomers displaced many of the Italian residents who had already staked a claim to the neighborhood. According to Julio's father, neighborhoods are forever changing. "You can't be angry at her for not understanding, me entiende?" Julio thinks, "I do understand. Doesn't mean that it's all good. That no harm is done."

The Power of Fire

Fire plays a central symbolic role in the novel. The book opens with Julio completing his recent arson job. Even though the fires he sets are requested by the owners of the vacant buildings, Julio's participation signals a betrayal of or a lack of respect for the neighborhood he claims to love. Throughout his childhood, Julio's neighborhood was plagued by fires set by landlords looking to make money from the insurance settlement or seeking government funds to rebuild. Fires were so prevalent that often families were warned that their building would be torched, and children explained to their teachers that they would be missing school the following day. Fire marshals would arrive to see whole families waiting on the curb with their suitcases packed. Other times, families were not warned, perishing in the flames. Fire disrupted lives, displaced members of the community, and eroded often deeply forged neighborhood connections.

Fire touched Julio personally at the age of 16. His father had joined the church as an outlet for his music, and due to his talent the church grew. It moved to a larger space, and Julio's family rented an apartment above it; they spent a lot of time helping to fix it up. "I'm embarrassed to say it," Julio observes, "but those were wonderful days growing up, every moment was a Sunday afternoon." Still, "[m]ysteriously, like God Himself, at night, the church had somehow caught fire.... One by one, the buildings on that block were torched." The destruction of the church marks the moment when Julio loses his faith in Christianity: "It was from that day on that, for me, the word of God was never 'love' or 'light' but 'fire.'"

It is no coincidence, then, that Julio's Orisha, or god, is Changó, the source of fire and lightning. Papelito even calls him Hijo de Changó or "son of Changó." The book takes its title from this metaphor. Is the novel's title in reference to the fires that Julio sets? Or does it refer to the fire that Trompo Loco starts to gain his father's approval? Alternately, the title could refer to Changó himself, a vengeful god who repeatedly destroys Puerto Rican lives and families.

Discrimination

Discrimination, too, plays a large role in the novel. Quiñonez explores the politics of construction sites and the exploitation of illegal labor. The boss, who is never named, is racist, calling all the workers "tacos" and claiming that it is in their nature to steal. He does not understand why Julio would come to work when he has a social security number he can use to get someone else to do the labor for him. When the pipes are stolen from the job site, the boss docks the workers' pay, and because they are illegal, they have no recourse.

When Julio goes to meet Helen in the trendy new bar, a white patron approaches him immediately on entering, asking where he can buy drugs, presuming that the neighborhood's nonwhite residents traffic in drugs or know people who do. Recently arrived immigrants face their own set of challenges in the novel. Julio goes to visit Antonio, who lives in a small, bug-infested apartment with nine other men. Conditions are deplorable.

Julio feels misjudged by his neighborhood as well. Because he lives with his parents, has no girlfriend or wife, and is close friends with Papelito, a homosexual, he is believed by many to be gay as well. Because he is not a violent individual, he cannot protect Helen when she starts a fight. Community members project conclusions and qualities onto Julio without considering other explanations or the lack of awareness informing their slurs and prejudices.

On a similar note, Quiñonez addresses the machismo Julio sees in his neighborhood. When he drives the young woman seeking the surgical procedure that will simulate a virginal state, he understands it is because of unfair, double standards at work in the community. When he asks Maritza why she condones this surgery, she answers, "This is female genital mutilation. Of course I'm against it. It's really about control over women. But right now, I have a scared girl who if she doesn't bleed on her wedding night is going to get the shit beaten out of her." The young woman is desperate and chooses to have the operation, but even that choice is not without its risk or danger. "If you have sex with stitches, well, you'll fool your husband but you could die."

Helen is outraged by the way she is treated on the street in East Harlem. She associates with Maritza, because Maritza is working for equality. Many men in the community beat their wives and girlfriends, and there are several occasions where men are sexually irresponsible, cheating on their wives, molesting their daughters, and infecting them with sexually transmitted diseases.

Quiñonez also examines the effect of AIDS on the community. Many of its victims—prostitutes, the partners of the already infected, intravenous drug users and addicts—come to Maritza's church to testify. Maritza, the ultimate activist, will only award citizenship to those who have the disease, further underscoring its common presence and the secrecy that surrounds it.

Secrecy and Revelation

Secrecy and revelation play a large role in the novel. Julio is deeply concerned with notions of truth. He keeps Trompo Loco's true parentage from him. Papelito encourages Julio to confess to his mother how he made the money for the mortgage and to reveal the details and nature of the agreement he has with Papelito; but Julio lies to his parents and to Helen. When he finally confesses to her that he is an arsonist, she laughs, thinking he is kidding. Perhaps the most important secret in the novel is Julio's awareness that he will be forced to set fire to his own building, the source of his pride, hopes, and dreams. One of the qualities he finds most attractive about Helen is her ability to tell the truth, as she sees it, in her letters, which are "authentic, genuine and true."

The Evolving Role of Language

Another thematic concern in Quiñonez's novel is the evolution of language in the neighborhood. Julio speaks Spanish and English interchangeably, most often preferring to use Spanish. Quiñonez's narrative is peppered with Spanish phrases and words. A non-Spanish speaker can understand the phrases' meanings from their context, and it gives the reader a sense of the duality that everyone in the barrio lives with. At the job site, Julio's boss complains that it is "payday in my country and I want to hear English." But almost none of the employees speaks English.

As a result of the changes facing their neighborhoods, the residents of East Harlem forge a new language. Julio's family plays Spanglish Scrabble at home, creating words that exist in neither language but are imbued with meaning just the same. It is this new language, then, that helps them establish an identity and serves as a source of communication. This language is mirrored in the book itself, which, in its mixture of Spanish and English, challenges the traditional notion of an English-language novel.

JUNOT DÍAZ

Biography

JUNOT DÍAZ was born on December 31, 1968, in Santo Domingo, the capital of the Dominican Republic. At the age of seven, his family moved to New Jersey where he later became a U.S. citizen. When Díaz arrived, he was illiterate and barely knew his father, who had been working in the United States for years. His father soon left the family, and Díaz's mother worked in a chocolate factory to make ends meet. Díaz graduated from Rutgers University in 1992 and received his M.F.A. from Cornell University in 1995.

Díaz's big break came when his short story "Yisrael" was published in *Story* magazine in 1996. His debut collection of short fiction, *Drown*, won critical accolades and was published in Spanish as *Negocios (Businesses)*. While working on his writing, Díaz held a variety of jobs including dishwasher, steelworker, and assistant at a copy shop. Díaz's next piece of fiction took 10 years to emerge. *The Brief Wondrous Life of Oscar Wao* was published in 2007, to great acclaim. It won the Pulitzer Prize for Fiction in 2008, the United States' top prize for literature.

Though Díaz bears a resemblance to his characters, he insists that people should stop confusing the author with his fictive creations. Yet parallels exist. Like the main character in *Oscar Wao*, Díaz was working on a science fiction novel that he did not complete. It dealt with a postapocalyptic New York City and was viewed as inappropriate after the terrorist attacks on September 11, 2001. He considers science fiction to be his port of entry into writing: "As a kid I used to love this insane apocalyptic writer of children's stories, this writer named John Christopher.... In some ways he was writing these stories about the apocalypse, about young adolescent boys always finding themselves in a scenario where they're one of the last people on earth, and it was just such an awesome metaphor for how I felt in those days." He also considers himself more of a storyteller than a writer and feels that if he had not been such a voracious reader as a child, he might have gone into filmmaking.

Díaz thinks that the Latino experience is akin to science fiction: "So that if you're a person writing about a Dominican diasporic experience, to hew too closely to canonical ideal of what literature is would limit you. The conventions of what is canonically known as literature can't hope to encompass these radical experiences that you undergo when living in a diaspora like the Dominican one. And sometimes the only way to describe these lived moments—the surreality and ir-reality of some of the things that people like myself have experienced—is through lenses like science fiction." With these words, Díaz is suggesting that the experience of being transported from the Dominican Republic to the United States is almost like being teleported between time periods or planets. That is why Díaz is so drawn to the science fiction genre.

Díaz has won many awards including a Guggenheim Fellowship and a Rome Prize. He gained widespread fame when he was named one of the "New Faces of 1996" by *Newsweek* magazine. His work has appeared in *Best American Short Stories 1996*, *The New Yorker*, *Paris Review,* and *African Verse,* and he has written book reviews for *Entertainment Weekly.* Díaz currently teaches fiction at the Massachusetts Institute of Technology in Cambridge, Massachusetts, where he finds his love of science fiction (and science) shared. He has also been active in the Dominican community and has been a vocal spokesperson for immigration reform, condemning the illegal deportation of immigrants.

Drown
Summary and Analysis

Drown is a collection of 10 short stories. Alternately set in the Dominican Republic and immigrant neighborhoods in New Jersey, the stories often examine the coming of age of young men or the general immigrant experience itself. The first story, "Yisrael," centers on two brothers, 9 and 12, who are sent to the *campo* (countryside) in the summer when their mother works too many hours to look after them. They are bored in the country; Rafa, the older brother, lives to date girls but finds they are more willing to give him attention in the capital than in the country. One day, filled with boredom, the boys decide to travel to see Yisrael, a boy whose face was mauled by a pig when he was an infant. They have met the boy before—the narrator has hit him with a rock on the shoulder—but they have never seen his face.

The boys catch a bus, and Rafa manages to get them on without paying. On the bus, a man grabs the younger brother's genitals, and he begins to cry. The boys have to run off the bus to escape the fare collector and the driver. They find Yisrael and ask him to bring them to a store to buy a bottle of Coca Cola. Yisrael is a braggart. He wears a mask to cover his face and says that he is an expert wrestler.

He is going to the United States, he also claims, to have an operation to restore his face. The younger brother is intrigued by the story and by the boy. Yisrael wears clothing that his father has sent from the United States. He also knows a great deal about wrestling.

Rafa hits Yisrael with a bottle; they then tear his mask off. "His left ear was a nub and you could see the thick veined slab of his tongue through a hole in his cheek. He had no lips. His head was tipped back and his eyes had gone white and the cords were out on his neck." The boys leave him there unconscious and get on the first bus that passes. It is traveling in the wrong direction, and again they have not paid the fare, so Rafa tells his brother to get ready to run at the next stop.

In "Fiesta, 1980," Rafa and his brother, Yunior, have been living in the United States for three years. Together with their parents and younger sister, they are going to a welcome party for their aunt, who has just immigrated to the Bronx, New York. The problem is that every time Yunior gets into the family van he gets carsick. His father has no patience for his delicate stomach. He takes the boy on practice drives, in the hope he will overcome his persistent carsickness. On one such trip, his father took him to a woman's house so he could get cleaned up, while she and his father disappeared upstairs. Yunior told his brother what he had seen, and Rafa said that he had met the Puerto Rican woman too.

On their way to the party, Yunior's father gets upset because his mother fed Yunior, and he is sure to throw up. At the party, Yunior eats more and spends time with his cousins. At the party, custom dictates that the women stand in the kitchen and prepare the food. The children are the only ones who thank them. The adults then drink and dance, while the children play games and watch television. Yunior becomes worried that his father will be exposed as an adulterer in public. Yunior's aunt asks him about his parents' marriage, with Yunior asserting that nothing is wrong: "Maybe I already knew how it would all end up in a few years, Mami without Papi." All remains calm that evening, as the family piles back into the van to drive home; but Yunior's queasiness returns.

"Aurora" addresses the narrator's relationship with a heroin addict. The main character lives with his friend and business partner Cut. Cut does not approve of the narrator's relationship with 17-year-old Aurora, but the narrator says, "I can't help myself with her." They meet in the utility room to have sex; when he wakes up later, she is gone, after having turned his pockets inside out searching for money. Another time, he wakes up to find her kissing his roommate. He reveals that he has hit her, and she has attempted to stab him with a pen. He excuses himself by saying that everyone indulges in harmful actions, "stuff that's no good for you."

The narrator takes Aurora to meet a dealer and waits in the car. When an old man comes out, the narrator, taking his frustration out on a person he does not know, breaks the man's ankle. Then he remembers the time Aurora had just been released from a juvenile detention center. She came back to the narrator, skinny and nervous, talking about how she had survived in jail by imagining their life together: "kids, a big blue house, hobbies, the whole . . . thing." For a brief moment, the narrator can share in that dream.

In "Aguantando," Yunior is again the narrator. This story takes place in the Dominican Republic and describes the narrator's life before their immigration to the United States. Yunior lives with his brother, mother, and grandfather, in suspended animation, his mother accepting no suitors and waiting for his father's return. When Yunior's mother becomes too impoverished to support the family, she sends him and his brother away. Yunior spends his time at his godmother's house. She is more financially stable than his family and feeds him meat, which he rarely gets at home. Still, Yunior is always excited when his mother and brother arrive to pick him up.

One day, a man arrives and leaves again quickly on a motorcycle. Yunior's mother is upset but will not tell him why. His brother informs Yunior that their father wrote a letter saying he was coming for them but that they should not get their hopes up. Their father had sent another letter two years ago, and his mother had made a fool of herself, throwing a big party and buying the boys new clothes. When he did not show up, she was embarrassed and fell into a depression, leaving the boys with their grandfather and retreating to the country. Now, Yunior imagines their reunion: His father would be hesitant, not recognizing him, but would then look him and say his name, claiming him as his son.

In the collection's title story, the narrator is a young adult who lives at home with his mother, who tells him his friend Beto is home from college. So the narrator halfheartedly goes out to look for him. When he cannot find Beto, he goes to their old haunt, the community pool. Although it is closed for the night, a number of people have climbed over the fence to use the pool anyway. The narrator remembers how he and Beto used to steal clothing from the mall and recalls the time they got caught. He also reminisces about how Beto caught the bus every morning for school but goofed off all day.

The narrator's present reality is not inspiring. He and his mother live together in loneliness, barely speaking to each other. When he catches her on the phone with his estranged father, he hangs up. At night, he carouses with his friends. The only positive element in his life is his love of running, three or four miles every day.

The reason for the narrator and Beto's estrangement is eventually revealed. One night, after swimming, they went to Beto's house. His parents were out, and the two friends watched a pornographic movie, during which Beto slid his hand over and masturbated the narrator. The next night, it happens again. When a door slams in the apartment next door, they both jump, which makes the narrator realize they might get caught. He pulls on his clothes and never speaks to his friend again.

In "Boyfriend," the voice of the narrator changes over the course of the story, becoming increasingly slangy and using many Spanish phrases. The narrator eavesdrops on the woman who lives below him whose boyfriend is breaking up with her. He thinks about his own failed relationship with Loretta, who was cheating on him with a white stockbroker. The neighbor's boyfriend is cheating on her as well, as the narrator sees the man at the local bars.

The narrator thinks his neighbor is too attractive for him to date. He is obviously looking for a connection that he never shared with his old girlfriend. He claims to be impervious to pain, but it is apparent he is not yet over her: "I had heart-leather like walruses got blubber." One day he invites his neighbor up for coffee, and they share an awkward moment. They later pass on the stairs like strangers, and he continues to hear her crying about the breakup, which she eventually accepts. The next time he sees her she has cut her hair short. "You look fierce," he says.

In "Edison, New Jersey," the narrator delivers pool tables with his partner Wayne. They try twice to deliver an expensive table to a house in a new housing development. At first, no one is home, then a black woman peeks out but will not let them in. Back at the store, the narrator steals from the boss. He used to spend the money on his girlfriend, but she left him for a white man; now he saves the money, calculating how long it will take him to buy a pool table. When he is at other people's houses, he takes small things—razors, cookies. If they tip poorly or are rude, the narrator throws a wad of toilet paper to clog the toilet.

The next time the pair tries to deliver the table, the black woman lets them in. She is from the Dominican Republic, like the narrator, and they strike up a conversation while Wayne sets up the table. She asks them for a ride to New York City. She wants to leave the man she lives with. The narrator agrees to drive her. In the ensuing weeks, the narrator calls the man's house. On the fourth attempt, the woman answers, confirming his suspicion that she would return to the man. Sighing, Wayne and the narrator play a game in which the narrator guesses where tomorrow's delivery will be. He guesses Edison, New Jersey.

In "How to Date a Browngirl, Blackgirl, Whitegirl or Halfie," the teenage narrator gives the reader advice as he talks about how he prepares for a date. First, he lies to his mother about not feeling well so that she will go visit the narrator's sick aunt without him. Then, he will hide the government cheese, which would be a clue that he is poor. Then he will hide the embarrassing photos showing him with an afro or in a village in the Dominican Republic with a goat. He knows that no girl's parents want them to date a boy from the Terrace, his part of town, but he knows that the girl will convince her parents that she should go over to his house. If she is a local girl, he will not worry about the time. She will come "when she's good and ready."

Finally the girl will show up and say that her mom wants to meet him. He will relax. "Run a hand through your hair like the whiteboys do even though the only thing that runs easily through your hair is Africa." He will give the mother directions back to the main road. If the girl is from the Terrace, too, he will take her to a restaurant serving Hispanic cuisine. He will order in his "busted up Spanish" and let her correct him or be amazed at his ability to speak the language. If she is not a local resident, he will take her to a fast food resturant, regaling her with stories of the neighborhood's many colorful characters. Over dinner, a halfie (by which he means a mixed-race individual) "will tell you that her parents met in the Movement.... Put down your hamburger and say, It must have been hard." He will wonder how she "feels about Dominicans." Then he will take her back to his house to watch television. Local girls will not fool around. "She has to live in the same neighborhood you do ... she might ... give it up, but that's rare." Meanwhile, "a whitegirl might just give it up right then. Don't stop her.... Tell her that you love her hair, that you love her skin, her lips, because, in truth, you love them more than you love your own." But the date does not always end in intimacy. Some girls do not like their hair to be touched. They complain, "You're the only kind of guy who asks me out.... You and the blackboys." The goodbye will be awkward. He will put the government cheese back before his mother finds out.

The story "No Face" is told from Yisrael's point of view, the boy whose face was eaten by a pig and who appears in the first story. He is obsessed with wrestling and thinks he is a superhero with powers of invisibility, the ability to fly, and superhuman strength. He often hides from local bullies in the church where the priest tries to teach him to read and write. The priest, who is trying to get the boy to the United States for surgery, takes him to a clinic in the city where he meets a boy with a severe condition: his skull is incomplete, exposing his brain. Yisrael worries about going to the United States: "Do they like wrestling?" he asks. When his little brother asks him where he has been, he says he has been out fighting evil.

"Negocios" is the last and longest story in the collection, the story of Yunior's father, Ramón, in the years between his leaving the Dominican Republic and returning for his family. Ramón's marriage had already fallen apart; he is cheating on his wife when his visa is approved. He borrows money from his father-in-law and takes a plane to Miami where a kind cab driver helps him into the city. He gets a job as a dishwasher but soon grows annoyed at his roommate, who is overcharging on the rent. He hitchhikes to New York, catching a ride at one point with federal marshals. His visa expires, and he worries about being deported or, worse, robbed and jailed. He begins to sporadically send money back to his family in the Dominican Republic. He works 20-hour days and falls frequently ill. He meets with a woman, paying her $800 to marry him and make him a citizen, but the woman disappears with the money.

Then, one day, he meets Nilda, a citizen, in a laundromat, who agrees to help him with his English. Eventually, he moves in with her and her daughter. He stops sending money to the Dominican Republic and winces when he receives letters from his wife detailing the extent of their poverty. He marries Nilda and becomes a citizen. His friend Jo-Jo, a successful convenience store owner, constantly nags him to remember his duty to his first family, while he insists to Nilda that he no longer cares about them. When she demands to know why he is again sending money to the Dominican Republic, he says that one of his children has died; Nilda does not believe him. They have a son, whom they name Ramón, the same name as his son in the Dominican Republic.

Ramón senior gets a better job, though racism means he is given the worst shifts. The couple saves enough money to visit the Dominican Republic, but Ramón does not see his family while he is there. His relationship with Nilda starts to deteriorate, and he begins to spend nights with his friends from work. Yet, when he injures his back at work, Nilda takes care of him. They fight, it turns violent, he leaves for two weeks, she takes him back. When Ramón's friend gets him a job as a security guard in a housing development in New Jersey, Ramón begins to see "his first familia was the logical destination. He began to see them as his saviors, as a regenerative force that could redeem his fortunes." He slowly moves his clothing to his new apartment.

Years later, having come to the United States, the narrator visits Nilda in New York. He introduces himself as Ramón's son and recognizes similar features in the picture of Nilda's son. She explains that she still remembers the dream she had on the morning Ramón left her. "I thought I would never stop hurting. I knew then what it must have been like for your mother," she tells the narrator. The narrator imagines his father's actions on the day he went to the airport, to fly home to the Dominican Republic to get his first family.

Major Themes

These stories have two settings, roughly paralleling Junot Díaz's own experiences. Some are set in the Dominican Republic, against a backdrop of poverty and loneliness. The father is always absent from the narrative but a major character, nonetheless, as his absence is acutely felt. The other stories are set in New Jersey and New York, where the main character is frequently a teenager or a young man, living with his broken family in his new home. The narrator is either Yunior or someone just like him, lonely, adrift, and without purpose.

The Immigrant Experience

Because the fathers in these stories are so often absent, the sons step into that role, working to provide for the family or feeling responsible for the abandoned mother. Children, then, grow up too fast, and boys have to assume adult male responsibilities in the household, reversing traditional parenting roles.

With these concerns and realities weighting many of the stories, the reality of the immigrant experience emerges as the main theme of *Drown*. Díaz says, "But the real story is about diaspora, about Dominican families having to live in these worlds where parents are abroad, and their kids don't really know them. It's pretty much a story about families and brotherhood." This experience is one marked by loneliness and isolation. Immigrants in the book long for their homelands. They miss being able to speak the language they know, Spanish, instead of having to struggle with imperfect English. They miss their distant wives or their extended families.

Women in the book are often portrayed as victims. The men mistreat them, using violence or withholding money. Yet the women miss their spouses and partners. In many of the stories, the women take back cheating husbands or talk to supposedly estranged husbands whom they have sworn off dozens of times.

Even those characters who grew up in the United States feel lonely and alienated from society. Many of Díaz's main characters try to date women who only reinforce their feelings of worthlessness and inferiority. Díaz attempts to create this feeling in the reader as well. "And part of what I was trying to get at when writing this book is that, you know, I wanted everybody at one moment to kind of feel like an immigrant in this book, that there'd be one language chain that you might not get." To this end, the book is written nearly entirely in the first person. The characters use the vocabulary available to them. They speak in stream-of-consciousness sentences and use Spanish phrases or slang. The dialogue is not indicated by quotation marks, as though internalized thought and speech or the spoken word are one and the same.

Racism

Díaz's characters comment honestly about racism, both their own and the racism they experience. Many of the characters suffer from low self-esteem, brought on by feeling they are ugly or worthless to society. They often envy those who possess different physical features, and they often lose girlfriends to more successful white men. The main characters lose jobs to these same men or are pigeonholed into inferior positions because of their ethnic background. Ironically, though, the main character (who is nearly always Yunior) suffers because he does not look "Dominican enough." He does not fit in either in the United States or in his country of origin.

The Brief Wondrous Life of Oscar Wao
Summary and Analysis

Junot Díaz's novel, *The Brief Wondrous Life of Oscar Wao*, which won the Pulitzer Prize for Fiction in 2008, is a funny, street-smart story of a first-generation Dominican-American nerd. It is written in Spanglish-inflected slang-filled prose, full of references to J.R.R. Tolkien's *The Lord of the Rings*, C. S. Lewis's *The Chronicles of Narnia*, role-playing games such as Dungeons and Dragons, video games, modern music, anime movies, comic books, and the history of the Dominican Republic. The author provides footnotes and asides to relate the island's history and his own insights. Díaz is equally at home talking about Tolkien as he is about Rafael Trujillo (the former dictator of the Dominican Republic), ancient

Dominican curses, student shenanigans at Rutgers University, and secret police raids in Santo Domingo. Díaz is able to move easily among the two worlds his characters inhabit, the ghost-haunted motherland that shapes their nightmares and dreams and the United States (specifically New Jersey), the land of freedom, hope, and possibilities that they have fled to.

The novel is narrated by Yunior, Oscar's roommate at Rutgers University and former boyfriend of his sister, Lola. Yunior is an athletic, compulsive womanizer who alternates between trying to help transform Oscar and trying to avoid him. Yunior is far less saintly and intelligent than Oscar and far more average. Oscar's sister, Lola, also narrates the chapter about her. A third narratorial presence is the author himself. Through footnotes and asides, he traces the history of the Dominican Republic, Trujillo's police state, and the resulting effects it had on Dominicans. His voice emerges as a more observant and polished version of Yunior's prose.

The book begins with a prologue that explains the Dominican curse, or *fukú*. It came from Africa by way of the slave ships after Columbus discovered Hispaniola. The appearance of a faceless man signals the curse is about to be unleashed. Yunior comes to believe that Oscar's family suffers from a strong curse, because so many terrible things have happened to them. The curse can be undone by *zafa*, an animal totem, part mongoose and part lion, a figure likened to Aslan from *The Chronicles of Narnia*.

In chapter 1, titled "Ghetto Nerd at the End of the World," the protagonist is introduced: Oscar DeLeon Cabral, called Oscar Wao (pronounced "wow") after an unfortunate Halloween costume that was supposed to resemble Dr. Who but actually turned out to look more like Oscar Wilde (mispronounced as Wao), an Irish playwright and author in the late 1800s and early 1900s. As the author injects, "Our hero was not one of those Dominican cats everybody's always going on about—he was no home-run hitter or a fly catcher, not a playboy." Instead, Oscar is an overweight, self-hating dweeb and aspiring science fiction writer, who dreams of becoming "The Dominican Tolkien." High school was torture for the outcast. He is not athletic and loves "any movie or TV show or cartoon where there were monsters or spaceships or mutants or doomsday devices or destinies or magic or evil villains." He can write in Elvish (the elf language) and knows more about the Marvel comic book universe than its originator: "Dude wore his nerdiness like a Jedi wore his light saber . . . couldn't have passed for Normal if he'd wanted to." Even his two geeky friends, Al and Miggs, manage to get girlfriends their senior year in high school, but Oscar continues to fall in love with girls who will not give him the time of day.

His one glimmer of potential romance comes in the form of Ana from his SAT class, who unaccountably spends time with him but puts him in the dreaded "friend" category. She has an abusive older boyfriend named Manny, who is in the army, and she tries to let Oscar down gently. Oscar starts college at Rutgers that fall, and once there his life becomes a college version of high school. His sister,

Lola, is a "Big Woman on Campus," but that does not make his life any better. He entered and leaves college still a virgin and with no girlfriend.

At this point in the novel, Lola narrates her own story. It begins when her mother, Beli, first discovers she has breast cancer. Lola had always been a dutiful daughter, but after the diagnosis, she becomes a "Banshees-loving punk chick." Lola raises Oscar and does all the household chores. Beli recovers but has to work three jobs after her husband abandons her. Beli constantly scolds Lola and has no sympathy for her when she is sexually abused. Lola runs off with Aldo in September of her junior year of high school. She is still unhappy, however, and only stays with Aldo until November, when she calls Oscar to meet her. Oscar brings his mother, uncle, and aunt. Once again back in the family fold, Lola is sent to Santo Domingo to live with her grandmother, La Inca. Lola is happy in Santo Domingo. She goes to school, does well, joins the track team, and has a boyfriend named Max. Then, 14 months after her arrival, her mother comes to bring her back to New Jersey.

The novel then moves back in time to relate the adolescence of Oscar and Lola's mother, Hypatia Belicia Cabral, known as Beli. From 1955 to 1962, she lives an idyllic life in Bani with La Inca, going to school and working in their bakery. Still, Beli yearns for something else, a dissatisfaction that grows stronger as she grows older. When Beli is 13, La Inca secures her a scholarship to El Redentor, one of the best schools in Bani. Beli stands out, because she has darker skin and is less educated than most of the other students. Everyone shuns her. To make matters worse, she falls for Jack Pujols, the school's whitest and most handsome boy. He ignores her. Then, in the summer after her freshman year, she blossoms into a stunning young woman, and the boys begin to take notice. When she returns to school, she commands Jack Pujols's full attention, but he uses her only for sexual gratification. When they are caught together in the janitor's closet, he insists that it is all her fault and she is expelled from the school.

Beli takes a job as a waitress at a restaurant where a fellow employee convinces her to go to the nightclub La Hollywood. It is there that she meets the Gangster, the love of her life and the reason she flees to the United States. He tells Beli that he is a businessman, but he does not reveal his history of murder and robbery. He has ties to pre-Castro Cuba and is also working for Dominican dictator Trujillo. Beli falls in love with him. The Gangster is gone for long periods of time, a warning sign that she does not heed. When he finally takes her with him on vacation, it ends when a policeman comes for the Gangster and tells him he is wanted at the palace. He leaves, promising to send a car for her, but none arrives, and as Beli hitchhikes home, she sees a man with no face, the harbinger of fukú, the curse. Two days later, she discovers she is pregnant. Though she is happy, neither La Inca nor the Gangster approves.

The Gangster, it is revealed, is not only married but is the husband of Trujillo's sister. One day after a fight with the Gangster, Beli is walking in the park when she is grabbed by two men and taken to see the Gangster's wife. The woman informs her that the men are members of the secret police and that she will never see the Gangster again. As the officers try to push her back in the car, she again sees a man with no face.

When La Inca discovers her daughter's disappearance, she and her friends pray for Beli's life. Beaten nearly to death, Beli has her clavicle, five ribs, and her right leg broken in three places and her front teeth knocked out. One of her lungs collapses, and she has a bruised kidney and liver. The police take her to a sugarcane field and leave her to die, but her anger and La Inca's prayers keep her alive. Then a strange mongoose, with golden lion eyes and a black pelt, leads her out of the sugarcane. The animal tells her that, although she will lose this baby, she will have two more children.

Trujillo is assassinated, but his organization and son carry on his cruel policies. Beli is sent to New York. Until she boards the plane, she still entertains hope that the Gangster will come and save her, but she never sees him again. She takes stock of her qualities: She is young and beautiful but sour, distrusting, unskilled, and uneducated. Her only hope for success is to find a man. The one sitting next to her on the plane will be her third and final love.

Next, Yunior gives his version of Oscar's college years at Rutgers, interspersed with his own college career from 1988 to 1992. He meets Lola in college and, though he really cares about her, the relationship turns out to be merely a brief fling. By the end of Oscar's sophomore year of college, he falls in love with another beautiful young woman, Jenni, who miraculously, likes him as well, despite having a boyfriend. When Oscar walks in on them, he goes berserk and later attempts suicide. Yunior offers to live with Oscar to keep an eye on him while Lola goes to Spain for a semester abroad. The two discover they share a love of writing. Oscar is, nonetheless, a social pariah, weighing more than 300 pounds and talking "like a Star Trek computer."

At the center of the novel is the story of the fall of Beli's father, Abelard Luis Cabral. He was a surgeon who had studied in Mexico City in the mid-1940s and had considerable standing in his hometown of La Vega. The Cabral family was wealthy and well-respected in the community. Abelard actively tried to avoid the dictator, Trujillo, but would occasionally be invited to parties that Trujillo also attended. One of Trujillo's known cruelties was demanding that very young women have sex with him.

Abelard's fukú, or curse, began with a party that he was invited to attend—the invitation specifically demanding that he bring his wife and daughter along. Abelard fretted and prayed and, at the last minute, decides not to take his wife and oldest daughter. At the party, he makes a feeble joke that there were no bodies in the trunk of his car. Four weeks later, the doctor is arrested by the secret police under charges of "slander and gross calumny against the person of the President." The witnesses all lie, swearing that he added "Trujillo must have cleaned them out for me" to the end of his joke.

Two nights after the atomic bombs were detonated in Japan, the family of Dr. Abelard Cabal would change along with the entire world. Abelord's wife, Socorro, dreamed that the faceless man was standing over her husband and her children. Abelard was taken to a secret prison, where he was starved and tortured. Shortly after, Socorro discovered that she was pregnant with their third and final daughter, Beli. It was also rumored that the real reason that Abelard was imprisoned was because he wrote a thinly disguised novel about a dictator with supernatural powers who had installed himself on an island and who could send a curse to destroy his enemies. Whatever the root cause, in February 1946, Abelard was officially convicted of all charges and sentenced to 18 years in prison. All of their property was confiscated.

Two months after Beli was born, Socorro stepped in front of a speeding ammunition truck and was killed instantly. The daughters were divided among whoever would take them. The oldest daughter, Jacqueline, was taken to live with her wealthy godparents in the capital, while the middle daughter ended up with relatives. They never saw each other or their father again. Their head servant was fatally stabbed; Abelard's mistress was found dead in her apartment. Two years later, Jacqueline was found drowned in her godparents' pool, though it only held two feet of water. The middle daughter was killed in 1951, when she was struck by a stray bullet that flew down the aisle and hit her in the back of her head while she was praying in church. Abelard is said to have gone insane and died a few days before Trujillo was assassinated and that he was buried in an unmarked grave somewhere outside the prison.

Beli was born dark and sickly. She spent the first few years of her life moving between relations who did not want her. Eventually, she became a *criada*, or a servant, but she would skip work to go to school, upsetting the master of the house in which she lived. He poured a pan of hot oil on her naked back to punish her. She nearly died but recovered, after which they locked her in a chicken coop. Word reached Abelard's cousin La Inca, who was operating a string of successful bakeries. She believed the girl to be dead, like the rest of the Cabal family. When La Inca saw her, however, she knew that Beli was her cousin's daughter. She took her back to Bani and raised her as her own.

At this point in the novel, the narrative returns to Oscar. He graduates from Rutgers in 1992 and moves back home. He begins substitute teaching at his old high school and sends his stories and novels out to publishers, but no one is interested. The school is just as much a torture to him as a teacher as it had been to him as a student. He is the object of his students' ridicule, and his only friend is transferred out of the district. He has no other friends and no social life, Lola and Yunior having moved to New York. He identifies his depression as the result of his family's fukú, and he puts a gun to his temple and contemplates suicide.

After he has been teaching for three years, his mother decides it is time for the family to return to the Dominican Republic. Oscar has not been to the island in eight years and marvels that a whole new country is materializing atop the ruins of the old one. There are better roads, nicer vehicles, brand-new luxury air-conditioned buses and fast food restaurants. The biggest change is La Inca's bakery chain; she has moved to the capital and purchased a new house with the proceeds of her successful bakeries. Oscar decides not to return to New York with Lola but to stay in the Dominican Republic with his mother. His decision is cemented when he falls in love with La Inca's neighbor, a semiretired prostitute named Ybon Pimentel.

Ybon is an attractive middle-aged woman who had once been beautiful and had plied her trade across Europe before retiring to the Dominican Republic. She and Oscar strike up a platonic friendship, though Oscar is falling in love with her. His mother and La Inca warn him about her, begging him not to continue the relationship. They are furious that he stubbornly insists on pursuing it. Ybon tells Oscar about everything: her Dominican boyfriend, the *capitán,* and her foreign boyfriends, the Italian, the German, and the Canadian and how they each visit her in different months. He tells her about the one trip he took with his college buddies to Wisconsin for a gaming convention. He talks about his love for his sister, Lola, and what happened to her. He even talks about trying to take his own life. Ybon drinks to excess, prompting Oscar to call Clives, the evangelical taxi driver his family always used, to lead them home.

Despite the pair's growing closeness, Ybon refuses to have a romantic relationship with Oscar. She increasingly mentions her boyfriend, the capitán, telling Oscar that he is jealous, and suggesting that they should not spend so much time together. Oscar sees himself repeating his previous patterns of pining after a woman who does not love him. They find a bullet embedded in the front door as a warning, but instead of heeding it, Oscar continues to see Ybon.

One night, Oscar is driving behind Clives, on his way home, Ybon passed out next to him. At a roadblock, the police officers ask Oscar to step out of the car. At that moment, Ybon wakes up and asks Oscar for a kiss. He complies; it is his first kiss. The officers shine their flashlights into his face and behind them, he can see Ybon's boyfriend, the capitán. Oscar knows he is in real trouble.

The capitán punches Oscar and gives him to the two police officers to take care of. After reaching the canefields, the police discover that their flashlight is out of batteries, so they drive to a store, buy batteries, and then drive back to the canefields. Oscar considers escaping, but he is too afraid. The policemen take him deep into the canefields and begin beating him with their pistols.

The only reason Oscar is not killed in the field is that Clives secretly follows the men. After they have left Oscar for dead, Clives hears someone singing. A blast of wind rips through the cane, and Clives sees the wounded Oscar. Oscar recalls his dream in which a mongoose was chatting with him. His nose is broken, his zygomatic arch is shattered, he has a crushed seventh cranial nerve, three of his teeth are missing, and he has a concussion, leaving him unconscious for three days. La Inca and Beli pray over him; neither remarks on the similarities between the violent canefield episodes that Oscar and Beli miraculously survive.

On the third day, Ybon comes to see Oscar. She had been beaten also and tells him that she can never see him again, after which he returns to the United States with his mother and his uncle. Well again, Oscar borrows money from Yunior and goes back to the Dominican Republic, heading immediately to Ybon's house. She tells him to leave, but he replies that he loves her. She tells him to return to the United States and calls the capitán. Oscar goes to La Inca's house and refuses to leave, even after his mother, and then Lola and Yunior, arrive to try and convince him.

The two policemen return for Oscar. Clives begs the men to spare Oscar's life, but they just laugh. Staring out the window of the police car, Oscar hallucinates. He sees his entire family on a bus, including his dead grandfather and grandmother. The driver is the mongoose, and the other officer is the man without a face. It is at this moment that Oscar realizes he will die. He sends telepathic farewells to his sister, his mother, La Inca, and all the women he has ever loved, especially Ybon. Then the men march him into the canefield. He begs them not to kill him, because they will be taking a great love out of the world. The policemen wait respectfully for him to finish before they shoot and kill him.

Yunior and Lola go to the Dominican Republic to claim the body. They try to file charges, but nothing is ever done. A year later, Beli succumbs to a relapse of cancer and is buried next to her son. Lola breaks up with Yunior after he cheats on her. She meets a man in Miami, gets married, and has a child. Yunior continues to dream of Oscar, sometimes seeing him as the mongoose and sometimes as a man with no face. After ten years of feeling lost and aimless, Yunior straightens out his life. He lives in New Jersey and teaches composition and creative writing at Middlesex Community College. He is the epitome of the suburban middle-class dream: He owns a house, coaches baseball, works out regularly, and writes. His womanizing days are over; he is married to a woman he adores and who adores him. He still runs into Lola, and they talk about Oscar. Yunior fantasizes that one day Lola's daughter will come to him for the story of Oscar's life. He will take her down to the basement to see her uncle's books, games, manuscripts, comic books, and papers. At other times, Yunior worries that the family still suffers from the fukú. He reveals that Oscar sent some letters home before he died in which he described spending one weekend with Ybon and, thus, did not die a virgin. In the end he experienced, however fleetingly, the beauty of love.

Major Themes

Multidimensional Storytelling

Junot Díaz's book is a work on a grand scale. He has woven together issues of self-love and teenage angst with larger concerns of political oppression and immigrant heritage. Díaz's prose, both as Yunior narrating Oscar's life and as the author of the footnotes, is hip and quick. He uses contemporary slang and has created a style all his own, mixing Spanish, hip-hop slang, and standard English into a descriptive new language.

One of the reasons the book stands out in American fiction is because it merges so many genres. Like the Latin American novels of the 1960s, Díaz uses magical realism to enhance his story. Both Beli and Oscar see a talking mongoose, and everyone in the book accepts the fact that the family is cursed. They have each seen the man with no face. Díaz also incorporates footnotes into the text, a postmodern element made popular by the writer David Foster Wallace. The narrator of the book is Yunior (who may or may not be the same Yunior of *Drown*), but Díaz inserts himself into the story as the author of the many footnotes that supplement the main text. Sometimes, they add to the action, give additional information, provide historical details, or explain a reference to science fiction or a Dominican term. This creates a disjointed reading experience, where the flow of the main narrative is deliberately interrupted, suggesting no one narrative approach could possibly fully capture or relate any tale.

This disrupted text mimics the experience of the main character, Oscar. Yunior emerges as his foil or opposite by partially fulfilling the stereotype of the woman-chasing, macho Dominican male. Oscar, on the other hand, is nerdy, overweight, lacking in self-confidence, unable to attract any woman, and obsessed with science fiction. Díaz turns stereotypes, involving not only cultural groups but also intelligent social outcasts, on their head to create complicated characters.

Many of his characters are not who they at first seem to be. In the beginning of the book, Beli seems to be an overbearing mother. She and Lola yell at each other constantly, and Beli appears unreasonable and overly strict. When it is revealed that Beli was also a rebellious teen and underwent terrible hardships, she emerges as a rich empathetic character shaped by her past and her former suffering.

The Historical and Cultural Past

The Dominican Republic also plays a large role in the novel. Its history is explained in the footnotes so that the book reads as a history of the island as well as the story of just a few of its former inhabitants. Díaz describes the island so lushly that it seems as though it could have been paradise. This makes the tragedy of finding out about Trujillo's rapes and abuse even more poignant: "Homeboy dominated Santo Domingo like it was his very own private Mordor; not only did he lock the country away from the rest of the world, isolate it behind the Plátano Curtain, he acted like it was his very own plantation, acted like he owned everything and everyone, killed whomever he wanted to kill, sons, brothers, fathers, mothers, took women away from their husbands on their wedding nights and then would brag publicly about 'the great honeymoon' he'd had the night before. His Eye was everywhere; he had a Secret Police that out-Stasi'd the Stasi, that kept watch on everyone, even those everyones who lived in the States." The specific aspects of his viselike grip on the country are revealed in Beli's experience—her father's imprisonment, her orphanhood, her abuse and rape—and are thus brought that much more vividly to life for the reader.

Díaz's notion of fukú, or the curse that is believed to have destroyed Oscar's family, can be seen as the plight of Dominicans in general. The island is portrayed as historically cursed, its inhabitants the descendants of slaves, the victims of Trujillo, or immigrants too often joining the ranks of the urban and suburban American poor. Oscar and his mother believe in the man with no face, who may or may not be the devil. Lola considers their bad luck as just a realistic and expected component of life. Either way, Díaz opens a window onto the complex history of the Dominican Republic through the small intimate picture of one family's life tinged with both sorrow and love.

CHRONOLOGY

1928
- Piri Thomas is born.

1937
- Rudolfo Anaya is born in Pastura, New Mexico, on October 30.

1943
- Due to the labor shortage caused by World War II, the U.S. government contracts with Mexico to bring in "braceros" as temporary workers.
- Acting on racism and discrimination, Californians enter Hispanic neighborhoods looking for those dressed in zoot suits and beat them.

1948
- Esmeralda Santiago is born in San Juan, Puerto Rico, on May 17.

1950
- On March 27, Julia Alvarez is born in New York City.

1951
- Oscar Hijuelos is born on August 24 in New York City to parents who have emigrated from Cuba.

1954
- The U.S. Supreme Court rules, in the case *Hernandez v. Texas,* that Hispanics have suffered discrimination. The decision grants Hispanic Americans a legal basis to protest discrimination.
- Sandra Cisneros is born on December 20 in Chicago, Illinois.

1954–58
- The U.S. government launches Operation Wetback to find and deport illegal immigrants. Among the 3.8 million people deported, most without a hearing, are many U.S. citizens of Mexican descent.

1958
- Cristina García is born on July 4 in Havana, Cuba.

1959
- Fidel Castro seizes power as a result of the Cuban revolution.

1960
- The term *Chicano* is used to describe Americans of Mexican descent, in response to a struggle for equality and recognition of achievement.

1961
- The Bay of Pigs, an ill-fated invasion attempt by the United States, strengthens Castro's hold on Cuba.

1962
- United Farm Workers Union, led by César Chávez, is created.

1964
- The bracero program is suspended.
- The Civil Rights Act introduces affirmative action to the United States. Title VII of the act prohibits discrimination on the basis of gender, creed, race, or ethnic background and creates the Equal Employment Opportunity Commission (EEOC) to ensure enforcement.
- U.S. sanctions against Cuba begin.

1965
- The United Farm Workers (UFW) institutes a grape boycott.

1966
- The first college-level Mexican-American history course is taught.
- Ernesto Quiñonez is born in Ecuador, exact date unknown.

1967
- Following the example of the Black Panthers, the Brown Berets battle police discrimination and provide food, clothing, and education to Chicanos and others of Hispanic descent.

1968
- The United States caps immigration from the Western Hemisphere for the first time, though national quotas are declared illegal.

- La Raza Unida Party forms in Texas as the official political arm of movements begun by Chávez and the Brown Berets.
- Junot Díaz is born on December 31 in Santo Domingo, Dominican Republic.

1969
- Students at San Francisco State College demonstrate, demanding an ethnic studies department.
- El Movimiento Estudiantil Chicano de Aztlan (MEChA), an organization of college students, is founded.

1972
- Rudolfo Anaya publishes *Bless Me, Ultima*.

1974
- Congress passes a law ensuring bilingual education for students who do not speak English.

1975
- The Voting Rights Act of 1965 is extended to Hispanic Americans. Ballots must be bilingual in certain areas.

1979
- Political upheaval and violence in Nicaragua, El Salvador, and Guatemala lead many to seek asylum in the United States.

1980
- The U.S. government steps up attempts to find and deport undocumented immigrants.
- Fidel Castro announces that anyone who wants to leave Cuba can do so at the Peruvian embassy. Applications for refugee status soar.

1983
- Oscar Hijuelos publishes *Our House in the Last World*.

1984
- Sandra Cisneros publishes *The House on Mango Street*.

1989
- Oscar Hijuelos publishes *The Mambo Kings Play Songs of Love*.

1990
- *The Mambo Kings Play Songs of Love* wins the Pulitzer Prize for Fiction. Hijuelos is the first Hispanic author to be awarded the prize. The book is made into a movie starring Antonio Banderas and Armand Assante.

1991
- Vintage Press reissues Sandra Cisneros's *The House on Mango Street*.
- Sandra Cisneros publishes *Women Hollering Creek and Other Stories*.
- Julia Alvarez publishes *How the García Girls Lost Their Accents*, the first major novel written by a Dominican-American author.

1992
- Cristina García publishes *Dreaming in Cuban*. It is named a finalist for the National Book Award.

1994
- The North American Free Trade Agreement (NAFTA) between Mexico, the United States, and Canada goes into effect, amid much criticism.
- Julia Alvarez publishes *In the Time of the Butterflies*.
- Esmeralda Santiago publishes *When I Was Puerto Rican*, a memoir.

1996
- Junot Díaz publishes *Drown*. Stories from the collection appear in the *New Yorker* and *Best American Short Stories*.
- *America's Dream*, Esmeralda Santiago's first novel, is published.

1997
- Julia Alvarez publishes *¡Yo!*
- Cristina García publishes *The Agüero Sisters*.

1998
- Esmeralda Santiago publishes *Almost a Woman*, a continuation of her memoirs.

1999
- Though tourists are still prohibited, humanitarian workers and cultural exchange participants are approved for travel to Cuba.

2000
- Ernesto Quiñonez publishes *Bodega Dreams*.

2002
- Oscar Hijuelos publishes *A Simple Habana Melody*.

2003
- Hispanics are the nation's largest minority group comprised of 37.1 million people.
- Nilo Cruz, author of *Anna in the Tropics*, becomes the first Hispanic playwright to win the Pulitzer Prize for Drama.

2004
- President George W. Bush appoints Carlos M. Gutierrez to the position of secretary of commerce. He is the first of many Hispanic cabinet members appointed by Bush.
- Ernesto Quiñonez publishes *Chango's Fire*.

2005
- Alberto Gonzales is confirmed as attorney general of the United States.

2007
- Junot Díaz publishes *The Brief Wonderful Life of Oscar Wao*.
- Cristina García publishes *A Handbook to Luck*.

2008
- *The Brief Wonderful Life of Oscar Wao* is awarded the Pulitzer Prize for Fiction.

2009
- Sonia Sotomayor is confirmed as a justice of the U.S. Supreme Court, the first Hispanic member of the court.

ADDITIONAL READING

Anna in the Tropics by Nilo Cruz

This Pulitzer Prize–winning drama is set in a cigar factory in Florida in the 1930s. While Cuban immigrants roll cigars, a "lector" reads *Anna Karenina* to them to pass the time. As mechanization threatens to end their livelihood, the workers become inspired by Tolstoy's tale, creating an atmosphere of passion and jealousy that rivals the Russian novel.

The Ballad of Rocky Ruiz by Manuel Ramos

This first novel in a mystery series takes as its hard-boiled detective Luis Montez, whose alcohol consumption, along with his greedy ex-wife and own questionable past, are affecting his work as a lawyer. As a Chicano activist in the 1970s, Montez witnessed the murder of the activist leader Rocky Ruiz. When the other survivors begin to suffer mysterious misfortunes, Montez is forced to discover the truth about that night.

Before Night Falls by Reinaldo Arenas

This autobiography by Cuban and gay activist Arenas depicts his initial support for and later disillusionment with the Cuban communist government. Imprisoned for "ideological deviation" and for publishing work outside Cuba, Arenas is forced to denounce his own writing, finally escaping to the United States. The book was made into a film starring Javier Bardem 13 years after the author's suicide.

Borderlands/La Frontera: The New Mestiza by Gloria Anzaldua

The author uses multiple genres including prose fiction, poetry, and essay to weave a portrait of people caught between societies. Referencing myth, legend, and history,

Anzaldua creates an image of a Chicana who is neither Mexican nor American, as well as a lesbian who is never fully accepted in society.

Caramelo by Sandra Cisneros

Inspired by the author's childhood in which she was shuttled between Mexico and the United States, this novel's protagonist, Lala, frequently visits her grandparents in Mexico, where their privileged lives stand in sharp contrast to her family's poverty. In investigating and retelling her family's stories, a secret emerges that threatens their cohesion.

Days of Awe by Achy Obejas

Alejandra San José is an interpreter in Chicago who grew up in a Cuban community whose members are anxious for Castro's fall so they can return to their homeland. When her job takes her to Cuba, she learns that her family may have been *conversos*, Jews who converted to Christianity during the Spanish Inquisition. San José embarks on a quest to find out the truth about her ancestors and, along the way, herself.

Down These Mean Streets by Piri Thomas

This memoir chronicles the upbringing of a dark-complexioned Puerto Rican-Cuban American. Born into poverty in New York's Spanish Harlem, Thomas joins a gang, becomes a heroin addict, and ends up in prison. Throughout, he questions his identity as a Hispanic, at odds with his seeming African-American appearance.

Farewell to the Sea by Reinaldo Arenas

This novel is the third in Arenas's *Pentagonia* series, stories set in the wake of the Cuban revolution. In this installment, a poet, saddened by the results of the communist revolution he so longed for, sits on the beach contemplating his nation's recent history. His wife, too, mourns the loss of the Cuba she knows.

Loving Che by Ana Menéndez

An unnamed woman in Miami has been raised by her uncommunicative grandfather, who escaped Cuba with her when she was an infant. Throughout her life, her mother has been a mystery. When a box arrives from someone claiming to be her mother, the narrator begins to wonder if Ernesto "Che" Guevara might be her real father.

Nuyorican Poetry: An Anthology of Puerto Rican Words and Feelings edited by Miguel Algarin and Miguel Piñero

This 1975 anthology introduced American readers to the unique voices of Puerto Rican poets, who had been congregating and performing on New York's Lower East Side.

The editors, along with Jorge Lopez, Lucky Cienfuegos, T. C. Garcia, Americo Casiano, Bimbo de Ambulante, Martita Morales, Luz Rodriguez, and Shorty Bon Bon, contribute to this volume.

Revolt of the Cockroach People by Oscar Zeta Acosta

This novel is a thinly veiled account of the author's involvement in the August 29, 1970, Chicano Moratorium, a mass protest by Hispanics against the Vietnam War. Buffalo Zeta Brown is the attorney who represents the protestors, and the stress brought on by the high-profile case causes him to question his sanity.

Short Eyes by Miguel Piñero

This Broadway play tells the story of primarily African-American and Hispanic inmates at a prison in New York. When a white child molester joins their ranks, the prisoners threaten him (pedophiles, or "short eyes," are reviled in prison). The man confesses privately to Juan, who must then decide whether to snitch on a fellow inmate or allow the man to hurt other children when the case against him dissolves and he is about to be released.

Spirits of the Ordinary, a Tale of Casas Grandes by Cathleen Alcala

This novel weaves realism and magical realism into a multigenerational story of the Mexican-American border in the 1870s. The protagonists, Jews who practice their faith in secret, are influenced by infidelity, destiny, and the strange cliff dwellings called Casas Grandes.

Y No Se Lo Tragó la Tierra by Tomas Rivera

This novel, written in Spanish by the novelist, academic, and poet who typically works in English, is translated variously as *This Migrant Earth* or . . . *And the Earth Did Not Devour Him*. It is a stream-of-consciousness story told from multiple perspectives. An unnamed Chicano boy, the son of migrant workers, writes down his thoughts and observations, while the people around him add theirs in 14 vignettes. Collectively, the voices form a narrative portrait of one year in the boy's life.

Zoot Suit by Luis Valdez

This play, which debuted in 1979, was the first Chicano-authored play to appear on Broadway. Set against the backdrop of the Zoot Suit Riots and World War II, the play fictionalizes the true story of El Pachuco, a man thrown in prison for a murder he did not commit. Through the use of a newspaper reporter, musical interludes, and Pachuco (who functions as a Greek chorus, commenting on the action), the play examines the continuing racism Hispanics face in the United States.

BIBLIOGRAPHY

Books

Augenbraum, Harold, and Olmos, Margarite, eds. *U.S. Latino Literature: A Critical Guide for Students and Teachers.* New York: Greenwood Press, 2000.

———. *The Latino Reader: An American Literary Tradition from 1542 to the Present.* Boston: Houghton Mifflin Company, 1997.

Birmingham-Pokorny, Elba D. *An English Anthology of Afro-Hispanic Writers of the Twentieth Century.* Miami, Fla.: Ediciones Universal, 1994.

Calderón, Héctor, and José David Saldívar, eds. *Criticism in the Borderlands: Studies in Chicano Literature, Culture and Ideology.* Durham, NC: Duke University Press, 1991.

Christian, Karen. *Show and Tell : Identity as Performance in U.S. Latina/o Fiction.* Albuquerque: University of New Mexico Press, 1997.

Dalleo, Raphael, and Elena Machado Sáez. *The Latino/a Canon and the Emergence of Post-Sixties Literature.* New York: Palgrave MacMillan, 2007.

de la Campa, Román. *Cuba on my Mind.* New York: Verso, 2000.

Flores, Juan. *From Bomba to Hip-Hop.* New York: Columbia University Press, 2000.

Gilb, Dagoberto. *Gritos.* New York: Grove Press, 2003.

Gonzales-Berry, Erlinda, and Chuck Tatum, eds. *Recovering the U.S. Hispanic Literary Heritage.* Vol. II. Houston: Arte Público Press, 1996.

Gutiérrez, Ramón, and Genaro Padilla, eds. *Recovering the U.S. Hispanic Literary Heritage.* Vol. I. Houston: Arte Público Press, 1993.

Herrera-Sobek, María, and Virginia Sánchez Korrol, eds. *Recovering the U.S. Hispanic Literary Heritage.* Vol. III. Houston: Arte Público Press, 1999.

Kanellos, Nicolas. *Hispanic American Literature: A Brief Introduction and Anthology.* New York: HarperCollins College Publishers, 1995.

Padilla, Genaro. *My History, Not Yours: The Formation of Mexican-American Autobiography.* Madison: University of Wisconsin Press, 1993.

Pérez Firmat, Gustavo. *Life on the Hyphen.* Austin: University of Texas, 1994.

Romero, Mary, Pierrete Hondagneu-Sotelo, and Vilma Ortiz. *Challenging Fronteras: Structuring Latina and Latino Lives in the U.S.* New York: Routledge, 1997.
Saldívar, Ramón. *Chicano Narrative: The Dialectics of Difference.* Madison: University of Wisconsin Press, 1990.
Sánchez González, Lisa. *Boricua Literature.* New York: New York University Press, 2001.
Sommers, Joseph, and Tomás Ybarra-Frausto, eds. *Modern Chicano Writers: A Collection of Critical Essays.* New York: Prentice Hall, 1979.
Stavans, Ilan. *The Hispanic Condition.* New York: HarperCollins, 2001.
Tatum, Charles. *Chicano Literature.* Boston: Twayne, 1982.

Anthologies

Christie, John, and José González. *Latino Boom: An Anthology of U.S. Latino Literature.* Boston: Longman, Inc., 2005.
Gilb, Dagoberto. *Hecho en Tejas: An Anthology of Texas Mexican Literature.* Albuquerque: University of New Mexico Press, 2006.
Kanellos, Nicolas, and Kenya Dworkin y Méndez, et al., eds. *Herencia: The Anthology of Hispanic Literature of the United States.* Oxford: Oxford University Press, 2002.
Kanellos, Nicolas, and Ishmael Reed, eds. *Hispanic-American Literature: A Brief Introduction and Anthology.* Boston: Longman, 1995.
Ramirez, Luz Elena. *Encyclopedia of Hispanic-American Literature.* New York: Facts on File, 2008.
Rebolledo, Tey Diana, and Eliana S. Rivero, eds. *Infinite Divisions: An Anthology of Chicana Literature.* Tucson: University of Arizona Press, 1993.

Web Sites

Hispanic Heritage Month
http://www.hispanicheritagemonth.gov/

Identity Theory, an online magazine of literature and culture
http://www.identitytheory.com/

Latinoteca: The World of Latino Culture and Arts
http://www.latinoteca.com

The Nuyorican Poets Cafe
http://www.nuyorican.org/

Puerto Rico: 500 Years of Oppression
http://www.inmotionmagazine.com/puerto.html

Sandra Cisneros's Web Site
http://www.sandracisneros.com/

The Smithsonian Latino Center
http://latino.si.edu/

University of Minnesota, Voices from the Gaps: Women Writers and Artists of Color
http://voices.cla.umn.edu/

INDEX

A

"Aguantando" (Díaz), 97–98
Algarin, Miguel, 12
Almost a Woman (Santiago), 33–36
    cultural assimilation as theme, 36
    language and bilingualism as theme, 35–36
    movement/relocation as theme, 36
    summary and analysis, 33–35
    transitions of teen years as theme, 36
Alvarez, Julia, 38–52. See also *How the García Girls Lost Their Accents*; *In the Time of Butterflies*
    biography of, 39–40
    How the García Girls Lost Their Accents, 40–47
    major themes of, 46–47, 50–52
    photograph of, 38
    In the Time of the Butterflies, 10, 48–52
Anaya, Rudolfo, 18–25. See also *Bless Me, Ultima*
    biography, 19–21
    Bless Me, Ultima, 21–25
    major themes of, 24–25
    photograph of, 18
Arnaz, Desi, 56
"Aurora" (Díaz), 97–98

B

Bartheme, Donald, 55
Bless Me, Ultima (Rudolfo)
    dreams versus reality as theme, 25
    nature as theme, 25
    opposition and opposing influences as theme, 24–25
    preservation of innocence as theme, 25
    publication of, 20
    summary and analysis, 21–24
Bodega Dreams (Quiñonez)
    book 3: Bodega's death and legacy, 84
    cultural/historical legacies as theme, 85–86
    Hispanic New York as theme, 84
    moral ambiguity as theme, 85
    round 1: introduction to Sapo, 80
    round 2: Chino and Blanca, 80
    round 3: Chino and Sapo meet Nene, 81–84
    structure of as boxing match, 80
    violence as theme, 85
    writing of, 79
"Boyfriend" (Díaz), 99
Brief and Wondrous Life of Oscar Wao, The (Díaz), 102–110
    fall of Beli's father, 105–106
    "Ghetto Nerd at the End of the World," 103–104
    historical and cultural past as theme, 109–110
    Lola's narration of her story, 104
    multidimensional storytelling as theme, 108–109

Index **123**

multiple narrators in, 102–103
Oscar after Rutgers graduation, 106–107
Oscar and Ybon, 107–108
Oscar's adolescence with mother, 104
Oscar's death and aftermath, 108
prologue and *fukú*, 103
Pulitzer Prize in 2008, 102
Yunior's version of Oscar's college years, 105

C

Carlson, Lori Marie (Mrs. Oscar Hijuelos), 56
Castro, Fidel, 11
Catcher in the Rye (Salinger), 84–85
Chango's Fire (Quiñonez)
  book 1 summary, 86–88
  book 2 summary, 88–90
  discrimination as theme, 92–93
  fire power symbol as theme, 91–92
  gentrification and change as theme, 90–91
  language evolution as theme, 93
Chicano Renaissance, 12
Cisneros, Sandra, 62–67. See also *House on Mango Street, The*
  biography of, 63–64
  The House on Mango Street, 63–67
  major themes of, 67–67
  photograph of, 62
civil rights movement, 11
Columbus, Christopher, 9, 11
coming of age as theme, 32–33, 36, 46–47
Cuba, history of, 10–11
cultural assimilation as theme, 36

D

Dark Dude (Hijuelos), 56
Delgado, Abelardo, 12
depression and mental illness as theme, 75–76
Díaz, Junot, 94–110. See also *Drown* (short story collection)
  awards for, 96
  biography of, 95–96
  Drown (short story collection), 96–102
  photograph of, 94
  "Yisrael" (short story), 95

Diaz, Porfirio, 9
discrimination as theme, 92–93
diversity of viewpoints as theme, 15–16
Dominican Republic, history of, 9–10
Down These Mean Streets (Thomas), 12
Dreaming in Cuban (García)
  depression and mental illness as theme, 75–76
  memory power as theme, 74–75
  rebellion and revolution as theme, 75
  religion, spirituality, and supernatural as theme, 76
  section 1: "Ordinary Seductions, 1972," 70–72
  section 2: "Imagining Winter," 72–74
  section 3: "The Languages Lost," 74
  structure of novel, 70
  writing of, 69–70
dreams versus reality as theme, 25
Drown (Díaz)
  collection of ten short stories, 95, 96
  immigrant experience as theme, 101–102
  racism as theme, 102
  settings for, 101
  "Aguantando," 97–98
  "Aurora," 97–98
  "Boyfriend," 99
  "Drown" (title story), 98
  "Edison, New Jersey," 99
  "Fiesta," 97
  "How to Date a Browngirl, Blackgirl, Whitegirl or Halfie," 99–100
  "Negocios," 100–101
  "No Face," 100
  secrecy and revelation as theme, 93
  "Yisrael," 96–97
"Drown" (short story) (Díaz), 98

E

"Edison, New Jersey" (Díaz), 99
Empress of the Splendid Season (Hijuelos), 56
escape as theme, 15

F

family as theme, 15
feminism as theme, 14

"Fiesta" (Díaz), 97
fire power symbol as theme, 91–92
Fitzgerald, F. Scott, 84
Fourteen Sisters of Emilio Montez O'Brien, The (Hijuelos), 56
From When the World Was Good (Hijuelos), 56

G

Gadsden Purchase, 9
García, Cristina, 68–76. See also *Dreaming in Cuban*
    biography of, 69–70
    Dreaming in Cuban, 69–76
    Handbook to Luck, 70
    major themes of, 74–76
    Monkey Hunting, 70
    photograph of, 68
gender roles (dysfunctional) as theme, 66–67
gentrification and change as theme, 90–91
Great Gatsby, The (Fitzgerald), 84–85

H

Hijuelos, Oscar. See also *Brief and Wondrous Life of Oscar Wao, The*
    awards for, 55–56
    biography of, 55–56
    Dark Dude, 56
    Empress of the Splendid Season, 56
    The Fourteen Sisters of Emilio Montez O'Brien, 56
    major themes of, 60–61
    Mr. Ives' Christmas, 56
    Our House in the Last World, 55
    photograph of, 54
    Simple Habana Melody, 56
    The Mambo Kings Play Songs of Love, 56
    From When the World Was Good, 56
Hinojosa-Smith, Rolando, 12
Hispanic, defined, 7
historical and cultural past as theme, 50–51, 85–86, 109–110
histories, regional. See regional histories
House on Mango Street, The (Cisneros)
    gender roles (dysfunctional) as theme, 66–67

    publication of, 64
    strength and resolve as theme, 65–66
    structure of novel, 64–65
    word power as theme, 67
How the García Girls Lost Their Accents (Alvarez)
    awards for, 40
    coming of age as theme, 46–47
    Dominican experience as theme, 47
    identity, heritage, and culture as theme, 46
    summary and analysis, 40–45
    "Antojo," 40–41
    "Blood of the Conquistadores," 44
    "Daughter of Invention," 42–43
    "The Drum," 45
    "Floor Show," 43–44
    "The Four Girls," 41
    "The Human Body," 44–45
    "Joe," 41–42
    "The Kiss," 41
    "A Regular Revolution:," 42
    "The Rudy Elmenhurst Story:, 42
    "Still Lives," 45
"How to Date a Browngirl, Blackgirl, Whitegirl or Halfie" (Díaz), 99–100

I

I Love Lucy (TV show), 56
identity as theme, 12–13
immigrant experience as theme, 12
In the Time of the Butterflies (Alvarez), 10
    Dedé's story, 48, 49, 50
    historical past as theme, 50–51
    Mate's story (Maria Teresa), 48, 49, 51
    Minerva's story, 49
    Patria's story, 48–49, 51
    women's role in Dominican society as theme, 51–52
International Day Against Violence Against Women, 52

K

Kennedy, John F., 11

L

language as theme. *See also* Spanglish
    bilingualism and, 35–36

evolution of, 93
fluency and, 13
Latino, defined, 7
literary history, 11–12

M

Mambo Kings Play Songs of Love, The (Hijuelos), 56–60
    first section: recollections of past, 56–57
    love and intimacy as theme, 60
    music and language as theme, 61
    second section: Nestor's perspective, 57–59, 59–60
memory power as theme, 74–75
Mexico, history of, 8–9
Mirabel sisters' story, 10, 48–52
Monkey Hunting (García), 70
moral ambiguity as theme, 85
movement/relocation as theme, 36
Mr. Ives' Christmas (Hijuelos), 56
multidimensional storytelling as theme, 108–109

N

nature as theme, 25
"Negocios" (Díaz), 100–101
"No Face" (Díaz), 100
Nuyorican Poets Café, 12

O

opposition and opposing influences as theme, 24–25
Our House in the Last World (Hijuelos), 55
overview, 7–17

P

Parker, Gloria, 56
Piñero, Miguel, 12
poverty as theme, 13–14
preservation of innocence as theme, 25
Puerto Rico, history of, 11

Q

Quiñonez, Ernesto, 78–93. See also *Bodega Dreams*; *Chango's Fire*
    biography of, 79–80
    Bodega Dreams, 80–85

    Chango's Fire, 86–93
    major themes of, 84–86, 90–93
    photograph of, 78

R

rebellion and revolution as theme, 14–15, 75
regional histories, 8–11
    Cuba, 10–11
    Dominican Republic, 9–10
    Mexico, 8–9
    Puerto Rico, 11
religion, spirituality, and supernatural as theme, 76
Rivera, Tomá, 12

S

Salinger, J. D., 84
Santiago, Esmeralda, 26–37. See also *Almost a Woman*
    Almost a Woman, 33–36
    America's Dream, 27
    biography of, 27–28
    major themes of, 32–33, 35–36
    photograph of, 26
    Turkish Lover, The, 28
    When I Was Puerto Rican, 28–33
Short Eyes (Piñero), 12, 118
Simple Habana Melody, A (Hijuelos), 56
skin color as theme, 15
Spanglish
    cultural influences symbolized by, 13
    definition of, 8
    Juno Díaz's use of, 109
    as "new language," 84, 86, 93
strength and resolve as theme, 65–66

T

Teatro Campesino (Farm Workers Theater), 12
themes, common, 12–16. *See also specific themes* (e.g., gender roles)
    diversity of viewpoints, 15–16
    escape, 15
    family, 15
    feminism, 14
    hybridization of cultural influences, 13
    identity, 12–13
    immigrant experience, 12

language fluency, 13
　　　poverty, 13–14
　　　rebellion and revolution as , 14–15, 75
　　　skin color, 15
　　　violence, 14, 85
Thomas, Piri, 12
transitions of teen years as theme, 36
Trujillo Molina, Rafael Leonidas, 10
25 Pieces of a Chicano Mind (Delgado), 12

V
violence as theme, 14, 85

W
Wallace, David Foster, 109

When I Was Puerto Rican (Santiago)
　　　coming of age as theme, 32–33
　　　growing up in two worlds as theme, 32
　　　publication of, 27
　　　summary and analysis, 28–31
　　　women's role in Dominican society as theme, 51–52
word power as theme, 67

Y
Y no se lo tragó la tierra (. . . And the Earth Did Not Part) (Rivera), 12
"Yisrael" (short story) (Díaz), 95, 96–97
Young Lords (activist group), 79–80

PICTURE CREDITS

p. 18: Steve Snowden/Getty Images
p. 26: Newscom
p. 38: Ramon Espinosa/AP Images
p. 54: Ulf Andersen/Getty Images
p. 62: Ulf Andersen/Getty Images
p. 68: Newscom
p. 78: Stan Honda/AFP/Getty Images
p. 94: Ulf Andersen/Getty Images

ABOUT THE AUTHOR

A Chicago native, **Allison Amend** majored in comparative literature (Latin American and French literature) at Stanford University. She received an M.F.A. from the University of Iowa Writers' Workshop. Her fiction has received awards from and appeared in *One Story, Black Warrior Review, StoryQuarterly, Bellevue Literary Review, The Atlantic, Prairie Schooner,* and *Other Voices,* among other publications. She is the author of *Things That Pass for Love* (OV Books, 2008) and *Stations West* (LSU Press, 2010). Visit her on the Web at *www.allisonamend.com*